COOKIES
Bars & More

201 SCRUMPTIOUS IDEAS FOR SNACKS & DESSERTS

TASTE OF HOME BOOKS • RDA ENTHUSIAST BRANDS, LLC • MILWAUKEE, WI

Taste of Home

Reader's digest

A TASTE OF HOME/READER'S DIGEST BOOK

EDITORIAL

Editor-in-Chief: Catherine Cassidy
Creative Director: Howard Greenberg
Editorial Operations Director: Kerri Balliet

Managing Editor, Print & Digital Books:
Mark Hagen
Associate Creative Director: Edwin Robles Jr.

Associate Editor: Molly Jasinski
Art Director: Maggie Conners
Layout Designer: Catherine Fletcher
Editorial Production Manager: Dena Ahlers
Copy Chief: Deb Warlaumont Mulvey
Copy Editor: Joanne Weintraub
Content Operations Assistant: Shannon Stroud
Editorial Services Administrator: Marie Brannon

Food Editors: James Schend; Peggy Woodward, RD
Recipe Editors: Mary King; Jenni Sharp, RD; Irene Yeh

Test Kitchen & Food Styling Manager:
Sarah Thompson
Test Cooks: Nicholas Iverson (lead),
Matthew Hass, Lauren Knoelke
Food Stylists: Kathryn Conrad (senior),
Leah Rekau, Shannon Roum
Prep Cooks: Megumi Garcia, Melissa Hansen,
Bethany Van Jacobson, Sara Wirtz

Photography Director: Stephanie Marchese
Photographers: Dan Roberts, Jim Wieland
Photographer/Set Stylist: Grace Natoli Sheldon
Set Stylists: Stacey Genaw, Melissa Haberman,
Dee Dee Jacq
Photo Studio Assistant: Ester Robards

Editorial Business Manager: Kristy Martin
Editorial Business Associate: Samantha Lea Stoeger

BUSINESS

Vice President, Group Publisher:
Kirsten Marchioli
Publisher: Donna Lindskog

General Manager, Taste of Home Cooking School:
Erin Puariea
**Executive Producer, Taste of Home Online Cooking
School:** Karen Berner

THE READER'S DIGEST ASSOCIATION, INC.

President and Chief Executive Officer:
Bonnie Kintzer
**Vice President, Chief Operating Officer,
North America:** Howard Halligan
Chief Revenue Officer: Richard Sutton
Chief Marketing Officer: Leslie Dukker Doty
Vice President, Content Marketing & Operations:
Diane Dragan
**Senior Vice President, Global HR
& Communications:** Phyllis E. Gebhardt, SPHR
Vice President, Brand Marketing: Beth Gorry
Vice President, Chief Technology Officer:
Aneel Tejwaney
Vice President, Consumer Marketing Planning:
Jim Woods

For other Taste of Home books and products,
visit us at tasteofhome.com.

For more Reader's Digest products and information,
visit rd.com (in the United States) or rd.ca (in Canada).

International Standard Book Number:
978-1-61765-410-7
Library of Congress Control Number:
2014957264

Cover Photography: Lori Foy
Set Styling: Deone Jahnke
Food Stylist: Kathryn Conrad

Pictured on front cover:
Coffee Bonbons, page 197
Pictured on back cover:
Berry-Almond Sandwich Cookies, page 179,
and Coconut Citrus Bars, page 126
Illustrations on inside cover:
Ohn Mar/Shutterstock.com

Printed in China.
1 3 5 7 9 10 8 6 4 2

LIKE US
facebook.com/tasteofhome

TWEET US
@tasteofhome

FOLLOW US
pinterest.com/taste_of_home

SHOP WITH US
shoptasteofhome.com

SHARE A RECIPE
tasteofhome.com/submit

Loaded-Up Pretzel Cookies, page 15
Snow Angel Cookies, page 107

TABLE OF CONTENTS

The Family Cookie Jar........ 8

Classics With a Twist........54

Cute Creations 82

In the Pan....................112

Homemade Mixes 156

Holiday Faves................170

Indexes......................204

Secret Kiss Cookies,
page 81

Chocolate-Peanut Butter Crunch Bars,
page 136

COOKIE JAR CLASSICS & TASTY TREATS

Whether you like them crisp and buttery or soft and chewy, there's no denying the crowd-pleasing appeal of cookies. From classic Christmas cutouts to fast no-fuss nibbles, these blissful bites are a welcome addition to snack times, bake sales, coffee breaks, potlucks and lots of other occasions.

Now, baking up a batch of sweets is easier than ever with *Taste of Home Cookies, Bars & More*. Featuring 201 bite-size favorites, it's one book you'll turn to time and again. So what are you waiting for? Round up your gang and surprise them with a delicious new dessert or two today!

Find the Thick Su[...] Cook[...] on page [...]

Cookies 101

Before You Begin

Read the entire recipe and check to see that you have all the ingredients called for. Also make sure you understand the cooking techniques.

Preheat the oven for 10 to 15 minutes before baking. Use an oven thermometer to verify the accuracy of your oven. If the set oven temperature and the oven thermometer do not agree, adjust the oven temperature accordingly.

Get the Oven Ready

Position the oven rack so the baking pan will be in the center of the oven, unless the recipe directs otherwise.

Mixing It Up

Always prepare the ingredients before you start mixing. Let the butter soften, toast the coconut, chop the nuts, etc. Measure the ingredients correctly. Prepare the recipe according to directions

Avoid overmixing the cookie dough. If it's handled too much, the cookies will be tough. For even baking, always make cookies the same size and thickness.

Use heavy-gauge dull aluminum baking sheets with one or two short sides for cookies. For brownies and bars, use dull aluminum baking pans or glass. It's best to use the size of pan called for in the recipe

When a recipe calls for greased baking sheets or pans, grease them with shortening or cooking spray. For easy removal, line the bottom of the pan with parchment paper and grease the paper.

Unless the recipe directs otherwise, place cookie dough 2 to 3 in. apart on a cool baking sheet. For brownies and bars, spread the batter evenly in the pan, or the treats may bake unevenly.

While Baking

Leave at least 2 in. between the baking sheet or pan and the oven walls for good heat circulation. For best results, bake only one sheet of cookies at a time. If you need to bake two sheets at once, switch the position of the baking sheets halfway through the baking time.

Unless otherwise directed, let cookies cool for 1 minute on the baking sheet before removing to a wire rack. Cooling baked goods on a wire rack allows air to circulate around the food and cool it completely before storing.

Let baking sheet cool before placing the next batch of cookie dough on it. Otherwise, the heat from the baking sheet will soften the dough and cause it to spread.

MEASURE WITH PRECISION

1. Check liquid measurement at eye level.
2. Fill dry ingredients to the rim and sweep off excess with the flat edge of a metal spatula or knife.
3. Wet and dry ingredients should be filled to the rim of the spoon.

Storing Cookies & Bars

Cookies tend to change texture after storing—soft cookies get hard and cris cookies get soft. Here are some tips to keep these morsels at peak freshness.

- Allow cookies and bars to cool completely before storing. Cut crisp bar cookies while slightly warm. Allow icing on cookies to dry completely before storing.

- Store soft and crisp cookies in separate airtight containers. If stored together, the moisture from the soft cookies will soften the crisp cookies. Flavors can also blend during storage, so don't store strong-flavored cookies with delicate-flavored cookies.

- Arrange cookies in a container with waxed paper between layers.

- Store cookies in a cool, dry place. Cookies with a cream cheese frosting should be covered and stored in the refrigerator.

- If your crisp cookies became soft during storage, crisp them up by heating in a 300° oven for 5 minutes.

- Cover a pan of uncut brownies and bars with foil—or put the pan in a large resealable plastic bag. If the bars are made with perishable ingredients, such as cream cheese, store covered in the refrigerator. Once the bars are cut, store them in an airtight container in the refrigerator.

- For longer storage, freeze cookies or bars for up to 3 months.

- Wrap unfrosted cookies in plastic wrap, stack in an airtight container, seal and freeze.

- Freeze a pan of uncut bars in an airtight container or resealable plastic bag. Or wrap individual bars in plastic wrap and stack in an airtight container.

- Thaw wrapped cookies and bars at room temperature before frosting and serving.

Cream Wafers, page 13
Stacked Christmas Tree Cookies, page 199

Problem-Solving Pointers

Cookies Spread Too Much
- ☐ Place cookies on a cool baking sheet.
- ☐ Replace part of the butter in the recipe with shortening.
- ☐ If using margarine, check label and make sure it contains 80% vegetable oil.

Cookies Don't Spread Enough
- ☐ Use all butter instead of shortening or margarine.
- ☐ Add 1 to 2 tablespoons of liquid, such as milk or water.
- ☐ Let dough stand at room temperature before baking.

Cookies Are Tough
- ☐ The dough was overhandled or overmixed; use a light touch when mixing.
- ☐ Too much flour was worked into the dough.
- ☐ Add 1 or 2 tablespoons more shortening or butter or sugar.

Cookies Are Too Brown
- ☐ Check the oven temperature with an oven thermometer.
- ☐ Use heavy-gauge dull aluminum baking sheets. Dark baking sheets will cause the cookies to become overly brown.

Cookies Are Too Pale
- ☐ Check the oven temperature with an oven thermometer.
- ☐ Use heavy-gauge dull aluminum baking sheets. Insulated baking sheets cause cookies to be pale in color.
- ☐ Use butter, not shortening or margarine.

Bars Bake Unevenly
- ☐ Spread batter evenly in pan.
- ☐ Check to make sure oven rack is level.

Bars Are Overbaked
- ☐ Use pan size called for in recipe; too large a pan will cause batter to be thin and dry.
- ☐ Check the oven temperature with an oven thermometer.
- ☐ Check for doneness 5 minutes sooner than the recommended baking time.

Pastel Tea
Cookies

The Family Cookie Jar

PASTEL TEA COOKIES

These glazed sugar cookies are perfect for nibbling between sips at a tea party, graduation or shower.

—LORI HENRY ELKHART, IN

PREP: 1 HOUR + CHILLING
BAKE: 10 MIN./BATCH + STANDING
MAKES: 4 DOZEN

- 1 **cup butter, softened**
- ⅔ **cup sugar**
- 1 **egg**
- 1 **teaspoon vanilla extract**
- 2½ **cups all-purpose flour**
- ½ **teaspoon salt**
- 1¼ **cups confectioners' sugar**
- 2 **teaspoons meringue powder**
- 5 **teaspoons water**
  Pastel food coloring

1. In a large bowl, cream butter and sugar until light and fluffy. Beat in egg and vanilla. Combine flour and salt; gradually add to creamed mixture. Cover and refrigerate 1-2 hours until dough is easy to handle.

2. Preheat oven to 350°. On a lightly floured surface, roll out dough to ⅛-in. thickness. Cut with floured 2½-in. butterfly or flower cookie cutters. Place 1 in. apart on ungreased baking sheets.

3. Bake 8-10 minutes or until edges are lightly browned. Remove to wire racks to cool.

4. For glaze, in a small bowl, combine confectioners' sugar and meringue powder; stir in water until smooth. Divide among small bowls; tint pastel colors. Spread over cookies; let stand until set.

NOTE *Meringue powder is available from Wilton Industries. Call 800-794-5866 or visit* wilton.com.

BUTTERSCOTCH TOFFEE COOKIES

My cookie recipe, with its big butterscotch flavor, stands out at events among all the chocolate. I like to enjoy it with a glass of milk or a cup of coffee. It's my fall-back recipe when I'm short on time and need something delicious fast.

—ALLIE BLINDER NORCROSS, GA

PREP: 10 MIN. • **BAKE:** 10 MIN./BATCH
MAKES: 5 DOZEN

- 2 **eggs**
- ½ **cup canola oil**
- 1 **package butter pecan cake mix (regular size)**
- 1 **package (10 to 11 ounces) butterscotch chips**
- 1 **package (8 ounces) milk chocolate English toffee bits**

1. Preheat oven to 350°. In a large bowl, beat eggs and oil until blended; gradually add cake mix and mix well. Fold in chips and toffee bits.

2. Drop by tablespoonfuls 2 in. apart onto greased baking sheets. Bake 10-12 minutes or until golden brown. Cool 1 minute before removing to wire racks.

QUADRUPLE CHOCOLATE CHUNK COOKIES

Of all my recipes, I knew my Quadruple Chocolate Chunk Cookies would have the best shot of winning a cookie contest I entered. When your cookies feature Oreos, candy bars and all the other goodies that go into these treats, you can't go wrong!

—**JEFF KING** DULUTH, MN

PREP: 25 MIN. • **BAKE:** 10 MIN./BATCH
MAKES: 8 DOZEN

- 1 **cup butter, softened**
- 1 **cup sugar**
- 1 **cup packed brown sugar**
- 2 **eggs**
- 2 **teaspoons vanilla extract**
- 2½ **cups all-purpose flour**
- ¾ **cup Dutch-processed cocoa**
- 1 **teaspoon baking soda**
- ¼ **teaspoon salt**
- 1 **cup white baking chips, chopped**
- 1 **cup semisweet chocolate chips, chopped**
- 1 **cup chopped Oreo cookies (about 10 cookies)**
- 1 **Hershey's Cookies 'n' Creme candy bar (1.55 ounces), chopped**

1. Preheat oven to 375°. In a large bowl cream butter, sugar and brown sugar until light and fluffy. Beat in eggs and vanilla. In another bowl, whisk flour, cocoa, baking soda and salt; gradually beat into creamed mixture. Stir in remaining ingredients.

2. Drop by tablespoonfuls 2 in. apart onto greased baking sheets. Bake 6-8 minutes or until set. Cool on pans 1 minute. Remove to wire racks to cool completely. Store in an airtight container.

> I used to make these cookies as simple Christmas cutouts until I came up with the idea of adding a brown butter filling. Sometimes I'll fill the centers with melted chocolate.
>
> —**ALICE LE DUC** CEDARBURG, WI

BUTTERCUPS

PREP: 25 MIN. + CHILLING
BAKE: 10 MIN./BATCH + COOLING
MAKES: 3 DOZEN

- 1 **cup butter, softened**
- 1½ **cups confectioners' sugar**
- 1 **egg**
- 1 **teaspoon vanilla extract**
- 2½ **cups all-purpose flour**

FILLING

- ¼ **cup butter, cubed**
- 1½ **cups confectioners' sugar**
- ¾ **teaspoon vanilla extract**
- 5 **tablespoons water**
- ¼ **cup raspberry preserves or fruit preserves of your choice**

1. In a large bowl, cream butter and sugar until light and fluffy. Beat in egg and vanilla. Gradually add flour and mix well. Divide dough in half; wrap each portion in plastic wrap. Refrigerate 2 hours or until easy to handle.

2. Preheat oven to 375°. On a lightly floured surface, roll out each portion of dough to ⅛-in. thickness. Cut with a floured 2½-in. scalloped cookie cutter. Cut a 1-in. hole in the centers of half of the cookies with a floured cutter.

3. Place 2 in. apart on ungreased baking sheets. Bake 8-10 minutes or until lightly browned. Remove to wire racks to cool.

4. Heat butter in a small saucepan over medium heat until golden brown, about 7 minutes. Remove from heat; gradually add confectioners' sugar, vanilla and enough water to achieve a spreading consistency.

5. Spread on the bottoms of the solid cookies; top with remaining cookies. Place ½ teaspoon preserves in the center of each.

Cream Wafers

CREAM WAFERS

My sons used to help me make these cookies, and now my oldest granddaughter likes to lend a hand. Sometimes I can even convince the smaller grandchildren to join the fun! These cute sandwiches are tender, buttery and melt-in-your-mouth good!

—LINDA CLINKENBEARD VINCENNES, IN

PREP: 25 MIN. + CHILLING
BAKE: 10 MIN./BATCH + COOLING
MAKES: 2 DOZEN

- ½ cup butter, softened
- 1 cup all-purpose flour
- 3 tablespoons heavy whipping cream
  Sugar

FILLING

- ¼ cup butter, softened
- ¾ cup confectioners' sugar
- ½ teaspoon vanilla extract
- 1½ to 2 teaspoons heavy whipping cream
- 1 drop each red and green food coloring

1. In a small bowl, beat butter, flour and cream. Cover and refrigerate 1 hour or until easy to handle.

2. Preheat oven to 375°. On a lightly floured surface, roll out dough to ⅛-in. thickness. Cut with a floured 1¼-in. round cookie cutter. Place 1 in. apart on ungreased baking sheets. Sprinkle with sugar. Prick each cookie 3-4 times with a fork.

3. Bake 7-9 minutes or until set. Remove to wire racks to cool.

4. In a small bowl, combine butter, confectioners' sugar, vanilla and enough cream to achieve desired consistency. Remove half to another bowl; tint one portion of filling with red food coloring and the other half with green. Carefully spread filling on bottom of half of the cookies; top with remaining cookies.

JUMBO CHOCOLATE CHIP COOKIES

These huge cookies are a family favorite. No one can resist their sweet chocolaty taste.

—LORI SPORER OAKLEY, KS

PREP: 15 MIN. + CHILLING
BAKE: 15 MIN./BATCH
MAKES: 2 DOZEN

- ⅔ cup shortening
- ⅔ cup butter, softened
- 1 cup sugar
- 1 cup packed brown sugar
- 2 eggs
- 2 teaspoons vanilla extract
- 3½ cups all-purpose flour
- 1 teaspoon baking soda
- 1 teaspoon salt
- 2 cups (12 ounces) semisweet chocolate chips
- 1 cup chopped pecans

In a large bowl, cream shortening, butter and sugars until light and fluffy. Beat in eggs and vanilla. Combine flour, baking soda and salt; add to creamed mixture and mix well. Fold in chocolate chips and pecans. Chill for at least 1 hour. Preheat oven to 375°. Drop dough by ¼ cupfuls 2 in. apart onto greased baking sheets. Bake 13-15 minutes or until golden brown. Cool 5 minutes before removing to wire racks.

PISTACHIO CHOCOLATE MACARONS

Traditional macarons are confections made with egg whites, sugar and almonds. This version calls for pistachios instead of the usual almonds and features a luscious chocolate filling.

—TASTE OF HOME TEST KITCHEN

PREP: 35 MIN.
BAKE: 10 MIN./BATCH + COOLING
MAKES: ABOUT 1½ DOZEN

- **3   egg whites**
- **1¼ cups confectioners' sugar**
- **¾   cup pistachios**
-     **Dash salt**
- **¼   cup sugar**

CHOCOLATE FILLING

- **4   ounces bittersweet chocolate, chopped**
- **½   cup heavy whipping cream**
- **2   teaspoons corn syrup**
- **1   tablespoon butter**

1. Place egg whites in a small bowl; let stand at room temperature for 30 minutes. Line baking sheets with parchment paper; set aside. Place confectioners' sugar and pistachios in a food processor. Cover and process until pistachios become a fine powder.

2. Preheat oven to 350°. Add salt to egg whites; beat on medium speed until soft peaks form. Gradually add sugar, 1 tablespoon at a time, beating on high until stiff peaks form. Fold in pistachio mixture.

3. Place mixture in a heavy-duty resealable plastic bag; cut a small hole in a corner of bag. Pipe 1-in.-diameter cookies 1 in. apart onto prepared baking sheets. Bake 10-12 minutes or until lightly browned and firm to the touch. Cool completely on pans on wire racks.

4. Place chocolate in a small bowl. In a small saucepan, bring cream and corn syrup just to a boil. Pour over chocolate; whisk until smooth. Whisk in butter. Cool, stirring occasionally, to room temperature or until filling reaches a spreading consistency, about 45 minutes. Spread on the bottoms of half of the cookies; top with remaining cookies.

WRAP THEM UP!

For a decorative (and tasty) gift, wrap some cookies up in cellophane, place a bow on top and then tuck the package into a festive coffee mug.

LOADED-UP PRETZEL COOKIES

Coconut, M&M's and salty, crunchy pretzels make these loaded cookies unlike any you've ever tasted.

—JACKIE RUCKWARDT
COTTAGE GROVE, OR

PREP: 20 MIN. • **BAKE:** 15 MIN./BATCH
MAKES: 2 DOZEN

- 1 **cup butter, softened**
- 1 **cup sugar**
- 1 **cup packed brown sugar**
- 2 **eggs**
- 2 **teaspoons vanilla extract**
- 2½ **cups all-purpose flour**
- 1 **teaspoon baking powder**
- 1 **teaspoon baking soda**
- 1 **teaspoon salt**
- 2 **cups miniature pretzels, broken**
- 1½ **cups flaked coconut**
- 1½ **cups milk chocolate M&M's**

1. Preheat oven to 350°. In a large bowl, cream butter and sugars until light and fluffy. Beat in eggs and vanilla. In another bowl, whisk flour, baking powder, baking soda and salt; gradually beat into creamed mixture. Stir in remaining ingredients.

2. Shape ¼ cupfuls of dough into balls; place 3 in. apart on ungreased baking sheets. Bake 12-14 minutes or until golden brown. Remove from pans to wire racks to cool.

NOTE *To make smaller cookies, shape rounded tablespoons of dough into balls. Bake as directed.*

BUTTERY POTATO CHIP COOKIES

Can't decide whether to bring chips or cookies to a tailgate or party? These crisp and buttery cookies make plenty for the crowd and will keep people guessing the secret ingredient.

—RACHEL ROBERTS LEMOORE, CA

PREP: 15 MIN. • **BAKE:** 10 MIN./BATCH
MAKES: 4½ DOZEN

- 2 **cups butter, softened**
- 1 **cup sugar**
- 1 **teaspoon vanilla extract**
- 3½ **cups all-purpose flour**
- 2 **cups crushed potato chips**
- ¾ **cup chopped walnuts**

1. Preheat oven to 350°. In a large bowl, cream butter and sugar until light and fluffy. Beat in vanilla. Gradually add flour to creamed mixture and mix well. Stir in potato chips and walnuts.

2. Drop by rounded tablespoonfuls 2 in. apart onto ungreased baking sheets. Bake 10-12 minutes or until lightly browned. Cool 2 minutes before removing from pans to wire racks.

CHOCOLATE ORANGE CHECKERBOARD COOKIES

I use these for gifts during the holidays because I like the elegant flavor combination of chocolate and orange. The shortbread texture melts in your mouth, and the walnuts add a nice crunch.

—SANDY PAIGE LANDSTUHL, GERMANY

PREP: 30 MIN. + CHILLING
BAKE: 10 MIN./BATCH
MAKES: ABOUT 3½ DOZEN

- 1¼ **cups butter, softened**
- 1½ **cups confectioners' sugar**
- ¼ **teaspoon salt**
- 1 **egg**
- 1 **teaspoon vanilla extract**
- 3 **cups cake flour**
- 1½ **cups finely chopped pecans**
- ¼ **cup baking cocoa**
- 1 **teaspoon grated orange peel**
- ½ **teaspoon orange extract**

1. In a large bowl, cream butter, confectioners' sugar and salt until blended. Beat in egg and vanilla. Gradually beat in flour. Stir in pecans.

2. Divide dough in half. Mix baking cocoa into one half; mix orange peel and extract into remaining half.

3. Shape each portion into a 5½x 2x2-in. block. Wrap each block in plastic wrap; refrigerate 30 minutes.

4. Unwrap dough; cut each block lengthwise into quarters, making four 5½x1x1-in. sticks. Switch two of the chocolate sticks with two of the orange sticks, forming two checkerboard blocks. Gently press sticks together to adhere. Rewrap in plastic wrap; refrigerate 2 hours or until firm.

5. Preheat oven to 350°. Unwrap and cut dough crosswise into ¼-in. slices. Place 1 in. apart on ungreased baking sheets. Bake 9-11 minutes or until set. Remove from pans to wire racks to cool

DIY CAKE FLOUR

Don't have cake flour on hand? You can make your own! For every cup of cake flour in a recipe, use 1 cup minus 2 tablespoons bleached all-purpose flour and add 2 tablespoons cornstarch. Keep in mind the finished product may differ slightly.

Chocolate Orange
Checkerboard Cookies

COCONUT CLOUDS

Coconut lovers will have extra reason to celebrate when they taste these cakelike drop cookies.

—DONNA SCOFIELD YAKIMA, WA

PREP: 45 MIN.
BAKE: 10 MIN./BATCH + COOLING
MAKES: ABOUT 5½ DOZEN

- ¼ cup butter, softened
- ¼ cup shortening
- 1 cup sugar
- ½ cup packed brown sugar
- 2 eggs
- 1 teaspoon coconut extract
- 1 teaspoon vanilla extract
- 1 cup (8 ounces) sour cream
- 2¾ cups all-purpose flour
- 1 teaspoon salt
- ½ teaspoon baking soda
- 1 cup flaked coconut, toasted

FROSTING

- ⅓ cup butter, cubed
- 3 cups confectioners' sugar
- 3 tablespoons evaporated milk
- 1 teaspoon coconut extract
- 1 teaspoon vanilla extract
- 2 cups flaked coconut, toasted

1. Preheat oven to 375°. In a large bowl, cream butter, shortening and sugars until light and fluffy. Beat in eggs and extracts. Stir in sour cream. Combine flour, salt and baking soda; gradually add to creamed mixture and mix well. Fold in coconut.

2. Drop by tablespoonfuls 2 in. apart onto lightly greased baking sheets. Bake 8-10 minutes or until set. Remove to wire racks to cool.

3. In a small heavy saucepan, heat butter over medium heat 5-7 minutes or until golden brown. Pour into a small bowl; beat in confectioners' sugar, milk and extracts.

4. Frost cookies; dip in coconut. Let stand until completely dry. Store in an airtight container.

TOASTING COCONUT

To toast flaked coconut, spread in a 15x10x1-in. baking pan. Bake at 350° for 5-10 minutes or until lightly browned, stirring occasionally. Or spread in a dry nonstick skillet and heat over low heat until lightly browned, stirring occasionally.

MY KIDS' FAVORITE COOKIES

When I made these cookies for my boys while they were growing up, it was a real challenge to keep them out of the kitchen long enough to let the treats cool. I still make these mouthwatering morsels for my grown-up boys today.

—ARDYS SMITH PALO ALTO, CA

PREP: 15 MIN. • **BAKE:** 10 MIN./BATCH
MAKES: 5 DOZEN

- 1 cup butter, softened
- ½ cup sugar
- ½ cup packed brown sugar
- 1 egg
- 1 teaspoon vanilla extract
- 2 cups all-purpose flour
- 1 teaspoon baking soda
- ½ teaspoon salt
- 1½ cups quick-cooking oats
- 1 cup flaked coconut
- 5 milk chocolate candy bars (1.55 ounces each)

1. Preheat oven to 350°. In a large bowl, cream butter and sugars until light and fluffy. Beat in egg and vanilla. Combine flour, baking soda and salt; gradually add to creamed mixture and mix well. Beat in oats and coconut.
2. Roll into 1-in. balls. Place 2 in. apart on ungreased baking sheets; flatten slightly. Bake 10-12 minutes or until lightly browned.
3. Break each candy bar into 12 pieces; press a chocolate piece into the center of each warm cookie. Remove to wire racks.
NOTE *This recipe was tested with Hershey's milk chocolate baking pieces.*

CHERRY BONBON COOKIES

This is a cherished recipe from my grandma. The cherry filling surprises folks!

—PAT HABIGER SPEARVILLE, KS

PREP: 15 MIN • **BAKE:** 20 MIN. + COOLING
MAKES: 2 DOZEN

- ½ cup butter, softened
- ¾ cup confectioners' sugar
- 2 tablespoons milk
- 1 teaspoon vanilla extract
- 1½ cups all-purpose flour
- ⅛ teaspoon salt
- 24 maraschino cherries

GLAZE
- 1 cup confectioners' sugar
- 1 tablespoon butter, melted
- 2 tablespoons maraschino cherry juice
  Additional confectioners' sugar

1. Preheat oven to 350°. In a large bowl, cream butter and sugar until light and fluffy. Add milk and vanilla. Combine flour and salt; gradually add to the creamed mixture.
2. Divide dough into 24 portions; shape each portion around a cherry, forming a ball. Place on ungreased baking sheets. Bake 18-20 minutes or until lightly browned. Remove to wire racks to cool.
3. For glaze, combine sugar, butter and cherry juice until smooth. Drizzle over cookies. Dust with confectioners' sugar.

COOKIE NOTES

_____
_____
_____
_____
_____
_____
_____
_____
_____
_____
_____
_____
_____
_____
_____
_____
_____
_____
_____
_____
_____
_____
_____
_____
_____
_____
_____
_____
_____
_____
_____
_____
_____
_____
_____
_____
_____
_____
_____
_____
_____
_____
_____
_____
_____
_____
_____
_____
_____
_____

PEANUT CHOCOLATE WHIRLS

The mouthwatering combination of chocolate and peanut butter is irresistible in these tender swirl cookies. My daughters and I have such fun making this recipe together.
—JOANNE WOLOSCHUK YORKTON, SK

PREP: 20 MIN. + CHILLING • **BAKE:** 10 MIN./BATCH
MAKES: ABOUT 3 DOZEN

- ½ cup shortening
- ½ cup creamy peanut butter
- 1 cup sugar
- 1 egg
- 2 tablespoons milk
- 1 teaspoon vanilla extract
- 1¼ cups all-purpose flour
- ½ teaspoon baking soda
- ½ teaspoon salt
- 1 cup (6 ounces) semisweet chocolate chips

1. In a large bowl, cream the shortening, peanut butter and sugar until light and fluffy. Beat in the egg, milk and vanilla. Combine the flour, baking soda and salt; gradually add to creamed mixture and mix well.

2. Cover and refrigerate for 1 hour or until easy to handle. Turn on to a lightly floured surface; roll into a 16x12-in. rectangle.

3. In a microwave, melt chocolate chips; stir until smooth. Cool slightly. Spread over dough to within ½ in. of edges. Tightly roll up jelly-roll style, starting with a short side. Wrap in plastic wrap. Refrigerate for up to 30 minutes.

4. Unwrap and cut into ¼-in. slices with a serrated knife. Place 1 in. apart on ungreased baking sheets. Bake at 350° for 8-10 minutes or until lightly browned. Remove cookies to wire racks to cool.

Peanut
Chocolate Whirls

GLAZED MAPLE SHORTBREAD COOKIES

While visiting friends in the United States, I always make sure to buy maple syrup and maple sugar, because they're the best I've ever had. You can decorate these delicious shortbread treats with sprinkles, or they're just fine as is.

—LORRAINE CALAND SHUNIAH, ON

PREP: 25 MIN. + CHILLING
BAKE: 20 MIN. + COOLING
MAKES: 1½ DOZEN

- 1 **cup butter, softened**
- ¼ **cup sugar**
- 3 **tablespoons cornstarch**
- 1 **teaspoon maple flavoring**
- 1¾ **cups all-purpose flour**

GLAZE
- ¾ **cup plus 1 tablespoon confectioners' sugar**
- ⅓ **cup maple syrup**

1. In a large bowl, beat butter, sugar and cornstarch until blended. Beat in flavoring. Gradually beat in flour.

2. Shape dough into a disk; wrap in plastic wrap. Refrigerate 45 minutes or until firm enough to roll.

3. Preheat oven to 325°. On a lightly floured surface, roll dough to ¼-in. thickness. Cut with a floured 2¾-in. leaf-shaped cookie cutter. Place 1 in. apart on parchment paper-lined baking sheets.

4. Bake 20-25 minutes or until edges are light brown. Remove from pans to wire racks to cool completely.

5. In a small bowl, mix confectioners' sugar and maple syrup until smooth. Spread over cookies. Let stand until set.

THUMBPRINT BUTTER COOKIES

Fill the thumbprint in the center of these goodies with any fruit preserves you like. The buttery little rounds add beautiful color to a platter of treats.

—*TASTE OF HOME* TEST KITCHEN

PREP: 20 MIN.
BAKE: 10 MIN./BATCH + COOLING
MAKES: 2½ DOZEN

- 6 **tablespoons butter, softened**
- ½ **cup sugar**
- 1 **egg**
- 2 **tablespoons canola oil**
- 1 **teaspoon vanilla extract**
- ¼ **teaspoon butter flavoring**
- 1½ **cups all-purpose flour**
- ¼ **cup cornstarch**
- 1 **teaspoon baking powder**
- ¼ **teaspoon salt**
- 3 **tablespoons apricot preserves or fruit preserves of your choice**

1. Preheat oven to 350°. In a large bowl, cream butter and sugar until light and fluffy. Beat in egg, oil, vanilla and butter flavoring. In another bowl, whisk flour, cornstarch, baking powder and salt; gradually beat into creamed mixture.
2. Shape dough into 1-in. balls; place 2 in. apart on greased baking sheets. Press a deep indentation in center of each with the end of a wooden spoon handle.
3. Bake 8-10 minutes or until edges are light brown. Remove from pans to wire racks to cool. Fill each cookie with about ¼ teaspoon preserves.

PEANUT BUTTER COOKIES

This treasured recipe is the only one my grandmother ever wrote down. When my mother was married, she insisted her mother jot it down for her. That was a real effort, because Grandma was a pioneer-type cook who used "a little of this or that" till it felt right.

—**JANET HALL** CLINTON, WI

PREP: 15 MIN. • **BAKE:** 10 MIN./BATCH
MAKES: 3 DOZEN

- 1 **cup shortening**
- 1 **cup peanut butter**
- 1 **cup sugar**
- 1 **cup packed brown sugar**
- 3 **eggs**
- 3 **cups all-purpose flour**
- 2 **teaspoons baking soda**
- ¼ **teaspoon salt**

1. Preheat oven to 375°. In a large bowl, cream shortening, peanut butter and sugars until light and fluffy. Add eggs, one at a time, beating well after each addition. Combine flour, baking soda and salt; add to creamed mixture and mix well.
2. Roll into 1½-in. balls. Place 3 in. apart on ungreased baking sheets. Flatten with a fork or meat mallet if desired. Bake 10-15 minutes. Remove to wire racks to cool.

Frosted Malted
Milk Cookies

FROSTED MALTED MILK COOKIES

My family loves anything made with malted milk, so I knew I had a hit on my hands with this recipe. These cookies are among our favorites!
—**NANCY FOUST** STONEBORO, PA

PREP: 40 MIN. • **BAKE:** 10 MIN./BATCH + COOLING
MAKES: 4 DOZEN

- 1 **cup butter, softened**
- 2 **cups packed brown sugar**
- 2 **eggs**
- ⅓ **cup sour cream**
- 2 **teaspoons vanilla extract**
- 4¾ **cups all-purpose flour**
- ¾ **cup malted milk powder**
- 2 **teaspoons baking powder**
- ½ **teaspoon baking soda**
- ½ **teaspoon salt**

FROSTING

- 3 **cups confectioners' sugar**
- ½ **cup malted milk powder**
- ⅓ **cup butter, softened**
- 1½ **teaspoons vanilla extract**
- 3 **to 4 tablespoons 2% milk**
- 2 **cups coarsely chopped malted milk balls**

1. Preheat oven to 350°. In a large bowl, cream butter and brown sugar until light and fluffy. Beat in eggs, sour cream and vanilla. In another bowl, whisk flour, malted milk powder, baking powder, baking soda and salt; gradually beat into creamed mixture.
2. Divide dough into three portions. On a lightly floured surface, roll each portion of dough to ¼-in. thickness. Cut with a floured 2½-in. round cookie cutter. Place 2 in. apart on parchment paper-lined baking sheets.
3. Bake 10-12 minutes or until edges are light brown. Remove from pans to wire racks to cool completely.
4. For frosting, in a bowl, beat confectioners' sugar, malted milk powder, butter, vanilla and enough milk to reach a spreading consistency. Spread over cookies. Sprinkle with chopped candies.

COOKIE NOTES

_____
_____
_____
_____
_____
_____
_____
_____
_____
_____
_____
_____
_____
_____
_____
_____
_____
_____
_____
_____
_____
_____
_____
_____
_____
_____
_____
_____
_____
_____
_____
_____
_____
_____
_____
_____

RANGER COOKIES

These golden-brown cookies are crispy on the outside and soft on the inside. Their tasty blend of oats, rice cereal, coconut and brown sugar is irresistible. You won't be able to eat just one!

—MARY LOU BOYCE WILMINGTON, DE

PREP: 25 MIN. • **BAKE:** 10 MIN./BATCH
MAKES: 7½ DOZEN

- 1 cup shortening
- 1 cup sugar
- 1 cup packed brown sugar
- 2 eggs
- 1 teaspoon vanilla extract
- 2 cups all-purpose flour
- 1 teaspoon baking soda
- ½ teaspoon baking powder
- ½ teaspoon salt
- 2 cups quick-cooking oats
- 2 cups crisp rice cereal
- 1 cup flaked coconut

1. Preheat oven to 350°. In a large bowl, cream shortening and sugars until light and fluffy. Beat in eggs and vanilla. Combine the flour, baking soda, baking powder and salt; gradually add to creamed mixture and mix well. Stir in the oats, cereal and coconut.

2. Drop by rounded tablespoonfuls 2 in. apart onto ungreased baking sheets. Bake 7-9 minutes or until golden brown. Remove to wire racks.

CHERRY-NUT COOKIES

Dotted with dried cherries and pecans, these slice-and-bake goodies look and taste special. The dough freezes very well, and for me, that's a must.

—AMY BRIGGS GOVE, KS

PREP: 30 MIN. + CHILLING
BAKE: 10 MIN./BATCH
MAKES: 5 DOZEN

- 1 cup butter, softened
- 1 cup sugar
- 2 eggs
- 1 teaspoon almond extract
- 3¾ cups all-purpose flour
- 2 teaspoons baking powder
- ¼ cup heavy whipping cream
- ½ cup dried cherries or cherry-flavored dried cranberries, chopped
- ½ cup chopped pecans

1. In a large bowl, cream butter and sugar until light and fluffy. Beat in eggs and extract. Combine flour and baking powder; add half to creamed mixture and mix well. Beat in cream, then remaining flour mixture. Stir in cherries and pecans.

2. Shape into two 8-in. logs; wrap in plastic wrap. Refrigerate 2 hours or until firm.

3. Preheat oven to 350°. Unwrap and cut into ¼-in. slices. Place 2 in. apart on greased baking sheets. Bake 9-11 minutes or until lightly browned. Cool 1 minute before removing from pans to wire racks.

CHOCOLATE-DIPPED ANISE BISCOTTI

Classic Italian biscotti cookies reach a whole new level when you add delicately licorice-flavored aniseed. Wrap them up for your friends and family to enjoy with a steaming cup of coffee.

—LESLIE KELLEY DORRIS, CA

PREP: 35 MIN.
BAKE: 40 MIN. + COOLING
MAKES: 3 DOZEN

- ½ cup butter, softened
- 1 cup sugar
- 2 eggs
- 2 teaspoons anise extract
- 2½ cups all-purpose flour
- 1½ teaspoons baking powder
- ½ teaspoon salt
- 1½ cups sliced almonds, toasted
- 2 tablespoons aniseed
- 10 ounces milk chocolate candy coating, melted

1. Preheat oven to 325°. In a large bowl, cream butter and sugar until light and fluffy. Beat in eggs and extract. Combine flour, baking powder and salt; gradually add to creamed mixture and mix well. Stir in almonds and aniseed.

2. Divide the dough in half. On a parchment paper-lined baking sheet, shape each portion into a 12x2-in. rectangle. Bake 25-30 minutes or until firm to the touch and the edges are golden brown.

3. Cool on pans on wire racks. When cool enough to handle, transfer to a cutting board; cut diagonally with a serrated knife into ¾-in. slices. Return to baking sheets cut side down.

4. Bake 6-7 minutes on each side or until golden brown. Remove to wire racks to cool completely. Dip each cookie halfway into melted candy coating, allowing excess to drip off. Place on waxed paper until set. Store in an airtight container.

Shortbread

SHORTBREAD

I live in the Midwest, but many of my family's favorite recipes come from New Zealand, where I was born. These cookies bring back warm memories of my childhood, and I'm going to make sure to pass them on to the next generation of my family—no matter where they live.

—MRS. ALLEN SWENSON
CAMDENTON, MO

PREP: 15 MIN. + CHILLING
BAKE: 10 MIN./BATCH • **MAKES:** 5 DOZEN

- 1 **cup butter, softened**
- ½ **cup sugar**
- ½ **cup confectioners' sugar**
- 2 **cups all-purpose flour**
- ½ **cup cornstarch**
- ½ **teaspoon salt**

1. In a large bowl, cream butter and sugars until light and fluffy. Combine flour, cornstarch and salt; gradually add to creamed mixture and mix well. Roll dough into a 15x2x1-in. rectangle; chill.
2. Preheat oven to 325°. Cut into ¼-in. slices; place 2 in. apart on ungreased baking sheets. Prick with a fork. Bake 10-12 minutes or until set. Remove to wire racks to cool.

WHAT'S IN A NAME?

Confused about the difference between confectioners' sugar and powdered sugar? They're the same thing! Some cooks use one name and some use the other, but *Taste of Home* recipes stick with the term "confectioners' sugar."

COCONUT DROP COOKIES

My mom added nutritious ingredients to recipes whenever she could. Full of nuts and oats, these crispy-chewy cookies are the perfect example.

—CATHY WILSON ST. GEORGE, UT

PREP: 25 MIN. • **BAKE:** 15 MIN./BATCH
MAKES: 5½ DOZEN

- 1 **cup shortening**
- 1 **cup sugar**
- 1 **cup packed brown sugar**
- 2 **eggs**
- 1 **teaspoon vanilla extract**
- 2 **cups all-purpose flour**
- 2 **cups old-fashioned oats**
- 1 **teaspoon baking powder**
- 1 **teaspoon baking soda**
- ½ **teaspoon salt**
- 2 **cups flaked coconut**
- 1 **cup chopped walnuts**

1. Preheat oven to 350°. In a large bowl, cream shortening and sugars until light and fluffy. Add eggs, one at a time, beating well after each addition. Beat in vanilla. Combine flour, oats, baking powder, baking soda and salt; gradually add to creamed mixture and mix well. Stir in coconut and walnuts.
2. Drop by rounded tablespoonfuls 3 in. apart onto greased baking sheets. Flatten slightly. Bake 11-14 minutes or until golden brown. Cool 2 minutes before removing to wire racks. Store in an airtight container.

GINGER-DOODLES

PREP: 25 MIN. • **BAKE:** 10 MIN./BATCH
MAKES: ABOUT 5 DOZEN

- ¾ cup butter, softened
- 1½ cups sugar, divided
- ½ cup packed brown sugar
- 1 egg
- ½ cup maple syrup
- 3¼ cups all-purpose flour
- 1 teaspoon baking soda
- ¾ teaspoon ground cinnamon, divided
- ½ teaspoon ground ginger
- ¼ teaspoon salt
- ¼ teaspoon cream of tartar
- ¼ teaspoon ground nutmeg

1. Preheat oven to 350°. In a large bowl, cream butter, ½ cup sugar and brown sugar until light and fluffy. Beat in egg and syrup. In another bowl, whisk flour, baking soda, ½ teaspoon cinnamon, ginger, salt, cream of tartar and nutmeg; gradually beat into creamed mixture.

2. In a small bowl, combine remaining sugar and cinnamon. Shape dough into 1-in. balls; roll in sugar mixture. Place 3 in. apart on ungreased baking sheets. Bake 10-12 minutes or until light brown. Remove to wire racks to cool.

> When I was a kid, both of my grandmothers taught me how to bake, and I've been doing it ever since. My brothers like snickerdoodles and I like gingersnaps, so these cookies make all of us happy.
> —BECKY TOTH HAVRE, MT

Ginger-Doodles

NOTE *Crystallized ginger is available in the spice section or the international food section in grocery stores.*

CHOCOLATE-PEANUT BUTTER CUP COOKIES

If you want to enjoy one of these fully loaded snacks the day after baking, you'd better find a good hiding spot.

—**CHRISTINE COLEMAN** ROCHESTER, NY

PREP: 25 MIN. • **BAKE:** 10 MIN./BATCH
MAKES: 4 DOZEN

- 1 **cup butter, softened**
- ¾ **cup creamy peanut butter**
- 1 **cup packed brown sugar**
- ½ **cup sugar**
- 2 **egg yolks**
- ¼ **cup 2% milk**
- 2 **teaspoons vanilla extract**
- 2⅓ **cups all-purpose flour**
- ⅓ **cup baking cocoa**
- 1 **teaspoon baking soda**
- 1 **cup milk chocolate chips**
- 1 **cup peanut butter chips**
- 6 **packages (1½ ounces each) peanut butter cups, chopped**

1. Preheat oven to 350°. In a large bowl, cream butter, peanut butter and sugars until light and fluffy. Beat in egg yolks, milk and vanilla. Combine flour, cocoa and baking soda; gradually add to creamed mixture and mix well. Stir in chips and peanut butter cups.
2. Drop heaping tablespoonfuls 2 in. apart onto ungreased baking sheets. Bake 8-10 minutes or until set (do not overbake). Cool 2 minutes before removing from pans to wire racks. Store in an airtight container

CRANBERRY SLICES

The holidays wouldn't be complete without a plateful of homemade cookies. These sturdy treats ship well as gifts.

—**STACY DUFFY** CHICAGO, IL

PREP: 15 MIN. + CHILLING
BAKE: 15 MIN./BATCH • **MAKES:** 4 DOZEN

- 1 **cup butter, softened**
- ½ **cup sugar**
- 1 **egg yolk**
- 1 **teaspoon vanilla extract**
- ½ **teaspoon salt**
- 2¼ **cups all-purpose flour**
- ½ **cup dried cranberries, chopped**
- 6 **tablespoons finely chopped crystallized ginger, optional**

1. In a bowl, cream butter, sugar, egg yolk, vanilla and salt until light and fluffy. Gradually add flour. Stir in cranberries and, if desired, ginger. Divide the dough in half; form each half into a 6x3x1-in. block. Cover with plastic wrap and refrigerate 3 hours or up to 2 days.
2. Preheat oven to 350°. Unwrap logs; cut the dough into ¼-in.-thick slices. Place on ungreased parchment-lined baking sheets. Bake 12-15 minutes or until edges are golden. Remove to wire racks to cool.

FUDGE-FILLED TOFFEE COOKIES

I combined three recipes to come up with a crisp cookie with a sweet fudge center. Flaked coconut and coconut extract add out-of-this-world flavor.

—KAREN BARTO CHURCHVILLE, VA

PREP: 25 MIN. + CHILLING
BAKE: 15 MIN./BATCH
MAKES: 5½ DOZEN

- ½ cup butter, softened
- ½ cup sugar
- ½ cup confectioners' sugar
- ½ cup canola oil
- 1 egg
- ½ teaspoon almond extract
- ¼ teaspoon coconut extract
- 1¾ cups all-purpose flour
- ½ cup whole wheat flour
- ½ teaspoon salt
- ½ teaspoon baking soda
- ½ teaspoon cream of tartar
- ¾ cup milk chocolate English toffee bits
- ⅔ cup chopped pecans
- ⅔ cup flaked coconut
  Additional sugar

FILLING
- 1½ cups semisweet chocolate chips, melted
- ¾ cup sweetened condensed milk
- 1½ teaspoons vanilla extract
- 1¼ cups pecan halves

1. In a large bowl, cream butter and sugars until light and fluffy. Beat in oil, egg and extracts. Combine flours, salt, baking soda and cream of tartar; gradually add to creamed mixture and mix well. Stir in toffee bits, pecans and coconut. Cover and refrigerate 1 hour or until easy to handle.

2. Preheat oven to 350°. Shape dough into 1-in. balls; roll in sugar. Place 2 in. apart on ungreased baking sheets. Using the end of a wooden spoon handle, make an indentation in the center of each.

3. In a large bowl, combine melted chocolate, milk and vanilla until smooth. Spoon 1 teaspoon into the center of each cookie. Top with a pecan half.

4. Bake 12-14 minutes or until lightly browned. Remove to wire racks to cool.

GIANT MOLASSES COOKIES

My family always asks for these soft and deliciously chewy cookies. They're also great for sharing as holiday gifts or sending to troops overseas.

—KRISTINE CHAYES SMITHTOWN, NY

PREP: 30 MIN. • **BAKE:** 15 MIN./BATCH
MAKES: 2 DOZEN

- 1½ cups butter, softened
- 2 cups sugar
- 2 eggs
- ½ cup molasses
- 4½ cups all-purpose flour
- 4 teaspoons ground ginger
- 2 teaspoons baking soda
- 1½ teaspoons ground cinnamon
- 1 teaspoon ground cloves
- ¼ teaspoon salt
- ¼ cup chopped pecans
- ¾ cup coarse sugar

1. Preheat oven to 350°. In a large bowl, cream butter and sugar until light and fluffy. Beat in eggs and molasses. Combine the flour, ginger, baking soda, cinnamon, cloves and salt; gradually add to creamed mixture and mix well. Fold in pecans.

2. Shape into 2-in. balls and roll in coarse sugar. Place 2½ in. apart on ungreased baking sheets. Bake 13-15 minutes or until tops are cracked. Remove to wire racks to cool.

PEANUT BUTTER-FILLED COOKIES

Anyone who likes peanut butter cups will really go for this recipe. Sometimes I give it an elegant finish by sprinkling confectioners' sugar over a stencil onto each cookie.

—**DIANE MILLER** MILLERSBURG, IN

PREP: 25 MIN • **BAKE:** 10 MIN./BATCH
MAKES: 2½ DOZEN

- ½ **cup butter, softened**
- ¼ **cup peanut butter**
- ½ **cup sugar**
- ½ **cup packed brown sugar**
- 1 **egg**
- 1 **teaspoon vanilla extract**
- 1¼ **cups all-purpose flour**
- ½ **cup baking cocoa**
- ½ **teaspoon baking soda**

FILLING
- ¾ **cup confectioners' sugar**
- ¾ **cup peanut butter**
  Additional confectioners' sugar

1. Preheat oven to 375°. In a large bowl, cream butter, peanut butter and sugars until light and fluffy. Beat in egg and vanilla. Combine flour, cocoa and baking soda; gradually add to creamed mixture and mix well.

2. In a small bowl, combine the confectioners' sugar and peanut butter. Roll into 30 balls. Shape tablespoonfuls of dough around filling to cover completely; place 2 in. apart on ungreased baking sheets. Flatten with a glass.

3. Bake 6-8 minutes or until set. Remove to wire racks. Dust with additional confectioners' sugar.

SOFT HONEY COOKIES

This old-fashioned cookie has a pleasant honey-cinnamon flavor and a tender texture that resembles cake. It's been a family favorite for years.

—**ROCHELLE FRIEDMAN** BROOKLYN, NY

PREP: 15 MIN. + CHILLING
BAKE: 10 MIN. • **MAKES:** 16 COOKIES

- ¼ **cup sugar**
- 2 **tablespoons canola oil**
- 1 **large egg**
- 3 **tablespoons honey**
- ¾ **teaspoon vanilla extract**
- 1 **cup plus 2 tablespoons all-purpose flour**
- ¼ **teaspoon baking powder**
- ¼ **teaspoon ground cinnamon**
- ⅛ **teaspoon salt**

1. In a small bowl, beat the sugar and oil until blended. Beat in egg; beat in honey and vanilla. Combine the flour, baking powder, cinnamon and salt; gradually add to sugar mixture and mix well (dough will be stiff). Cover and refrigerate for at least 2 hours.

2. Drop dough by tablespoonfuls 2 in. apart onto a greased baking sheet. Bake at 350° for 8-10 minutes or until bottoms are lightly browned. Cool for 1 minute before removing from pan to a wire rack. Store in an airtight container.

ANISE BUTTER COOKIES

Here in New Mexico, these cookies are known as *bizcochitos,* which means small biscuits. There are many variations of the recipe, which has been passed down through the generations. They're a beloved tradition around Christmas, at wedding receptions and other special celebrations. They're good by themselves or dunked in milk or coffee.

—MARI LYNN VAN GINKLE

SANDIA PARK, NM

PREP: 30 MIN. • **BAKE:** 40 MIN.
MAKES: 5 DOZEN

- 2 **cups butter, softened**
- 1¾ **cups sugar, divided**
- 2 **eggs**
- ¼ **cup thawed orange juice concentrate**
- 4 **teaspoons aniseed, crushed**
- 6 **cups all-purpose flour**
- 3 **teaspoons baking powder**
- ½ **teaspoon salt**
- 1 **teaspoon ground cinnamon**

1. Preheat oven to 350°. In a large bowl, cream butter and 1½ cups sugar until light and fluffy. Add eggs, one at a time, beating well after each addition. Beat in orange juice concentrate and aniseed. Combine flour, baking powder and salt; gradually add to creamed mixture and mix well.

2. On a lightly floured surface, roll out dough to ¼-in. thickness. Cut with a floured 2½-in. round cookie cutter. Place 1 in. apart on ungreased baking sheets.

3. Combine cinnamon and remaining sugar; sprinkle over cookies. Bake 12-15 minutes or until golden brown. Remove to wire racks.

LEMON POPPY SEED SLICES

My mom taught me to bake, and I use lots of recipes from her abundant collection, including this one.

—PAULINE PIRAINO BAY SHORE, NY

PREP: 10 MIN. + CHILLING
BAKE: 10 MIN./BATCH
MAKES: 5½ DOZEN

- ¾ **cup butter, softened**
- 1 **cup sugar**
- 1 **egg**
- 1 **tablespoon 2% milk**
- 2 **teaspoons finely grated lemon peel**
- ½ **teaspoon vanilla extract**
- ½ **teaspoon lemon extract, optional**
- 2½ **cups all-purpose flour**
- ¼ **cup poppy seeds**

1. In a large bowl, cream butter and sugar until light and fluffy. Beat in egg, milk, lemon peel and extracts. Gradually add flour and mix well. Stir in poppy seeds. Shape into two 8-in. rolls; wrap each in plastic wrap. Refrigerate 3 hours or until firm.

2. Preheat oven to 350°. Unwrap and cut into ¼-in. slices. Place 2 in. apart on ungreased baking sheets. Bake 10-12 minutes or until edges are golden. Cool 2 minutes before removing to wire racks to cool completely.

CHOCOLATE SANDWICH COOKIES

Our five kids love having these cookies in their lunch boxes and keep asking when I'll make them again. The recipe comes from a cookbook that was put together for one of our family reunions.

—**ANNE FRIESEN** MORDEN, MB

PREP: 25 MIN.
BAKE: 10 MIN./BATCH + COOLING
MAKES: 2 DOZEN

- 1 **cup butter, softened**
- 2 **cups sugar**
- 2 **eggs**
- ½ **cup heavy whipping cream**
- 1 **teaspoon vanilla extract**
- 3 **cups quick-cooking or rolled oats**
- 1¾ **cups all-purpose flour**
- ½ **cup baking cocoa**
- 1 **teaspoon baking powder**
- 1 **teaspoon baking soda**
- ¼ **teaspoon salt**

FILLING
- 2 **tablespoons cornstarch**
- 2 **tablespoons baking cocoa**
- ¾ **cup water**
- ½ **cup sugar**
- 2 **tablespoons butter**
- ½ **teaspoon vanilla extract**

1. Preheat oven to 350°. In a large bowl, cream butter and sugar until light and fluffy. Beat in eggs, cream and vanilla. Combine dry ingredients; gradually add to creamed mixture and mix well.

2. Drop by tablespoonfuls onto lightly greased baking sheets. Bake 10 minutes or until set. Cool on wire racks.

3. Meanwhile, in a small saucepan, combine cornstarch, cocoa and water until smooth. Stir in sugar and butter. Bring to a boil over medium heat; cook and stir 2 minutes or until thickened. Remove from heat; stir in vanilla. Cool. Spread on the bottoms of half of the cookies; top with remaining cookies.

WISHING COOKIES

According to our family, if you break a Wishing Cookie in three pieces and eat all three without speaking, your wish will come true.

—KATIE KOZIOLEK HARTLAND, MN

PREP: 20 MIN. + CHILLING
BAKE: 5 MIN./BATCH + COOLING
MAKES: ABOUT 6 DOZEN

- 1 **cup butter, softened**
- 1½ **cups sugar**
- 1 **egg**
- 2 **tablespoons molasses**
- 1 **tablespoon water**
- ½ **to 1 teaspoon grated orange peel**
- 3¼ **cups all-purpose flour**
- 1 **teaspoon baking soda**
- 1 **teaspoon ground cinnamon**
- ½ **teaspoon ground ginger**
- ¼ **teaspoon ground nutmeg**

ICING

- 1 **cup confectioners' sugar**
- ½ **teaspoon vanilla extract**
- 1 **to 2 tablespoons milk**

1. In a large bowl, cream butter and sugar until light and fluffy. Add egg, molasses, water and orange peel; mix well. Combine flour, baking soda, cinnamon, ginger and nutmeg; gradually add to creamed mixture, beating well after each addition. Cover and chill at least 2 hours.

2. Preheat oven to 375°. On a lightly floured surface, roll dough to ⅛-in. thickness. Cut into stars or desired shapes and place on ungreased baking sheets. Bake 6-8 minutes or until edges are lightly browned. Remove to wire racks to cool completely.

3. For icing, combine sugar, vanilla and enough milk to achieve a drizzling consistency. Ice cookies as desired.

DOUBLE-DRIZZLE PECAN COOKIES

These toasted pecan treats are a must with my family and friends every holiday. Drizzling them with both caramel and chocolate makes them doubly delicious and extra pretty on the cookie plate.

—**PAULA MARCHESI** LENHARTSVILLE, PA

PREP: 25 MIN.
BAKE: 10 MIN./BATCH + COOLING
MAKES: ABOUT 3½ DOZEN

- ½ cup butter, softened
- 1½ cups packed brown sugar
- 1 egg
- 1 teaspoon vanilla extract
- 1½ cups all-purpose flour
- 1½ teaspoons baking powder
- ¼ teaspoon salt
- 1¼ cups chopped pecans

CARAMEL DRIZZLE
- ½ cup packed brown sugar
- ¼ cup heavy whipping cream
- ½ cup confectioners' sugar

CHOCOLATE DRIZZLE
- 1 ounce semisweet chocolate, chopped
- 1 tablespoon butter

1. Preheat oven to 350°. In a large bowl, cream butter and brown sugar until light and fluffy. Beat in egg and vanilla. Combine flour, baking powder and salt; gradually add to creamed mixture and mix well.

2. Shape dough into 1-in. balls; roll in pecans. Place 2 in. apart on ungreased baking sheets; flatten slightly. Bake 8-10 minutes or until lightly browned. Cool 2 minutes before removing to wire racks to cool completely.

3. In a small saucepan, bring brown sugar and cream to a boil. Remove from heat; whisk in confectioners' sugar. Immediately drizzle over cookies.

4. In a microwave, melt chocolate and butter; stir until smooth. Drizzle over cookies. Let stand until set. Store in an airtight container.

EXTRA-SPECIAL CASHEW CRESCENTS

Everyone will love these nutty shortbread crescents, whether glazed or dusted with powdered sugar. Cashews add that extra special taste, making them simply scrumptious.

—PAULA MARCHESI LENHARTSVILLE, PA

PREP: 15 MIN. + CHILLING
BAKE: 10 MIN./BATCH + COOLING
MAKES: 6 DOZEN

- 1⅔ cups lightly salted cashews
- 1 cup butter, softened
- ¾ cup packed brown sugar
- ½ cup sugar
- 2 teaspoons vanilla extract, divided
- 1⅔ cups all-purpose flour
- ¼ teaspoon salt
- 2 cups confectioners' sugar
- 3 tablespoons 2% milk
  Chopped lightly salted cashews and additional confectioners' sugar, optional

1. Place cashews in a food processor; cover and process until finely chopped.
2. In a large bowl, cream butter and sugars until light and fluffy. Beat in 1 teaspoon vanilla. Combine flour, salt and chopped cashews; gradually add to creamed mixture and mix well.
3. Divide dough in half; shape each into a ball, then flatten into a disk. Wrap in plastic wrap and refrigerate 30 minutes.
4. Preheat oven to 375°. On a lightly floured surface, roll one portion of dough to ¼-in. thickness. Using a floured scalloped round 3-in. cookie cutter, cut a semicircle from one corner of the dough, forming the inside of a crescent shape. Reposition cutter 1¼ in. from inside of crescent; cut cookie, forming a crescent 1¼ in. wide at its widest point. Repeat with remaining dough. Chill and reroll scraps if desired.
5. Place 1 in. apart on ungreased baking sheets. Bake 6-7 minutes or until edges begin to brown. Cool 2 minutes before removing from pans to wire racks to cool completely.
6. Combine the confectioners' sugar, milk and remaining vanilla; spread or drizzle over cookies as desired. Sprinkle with chopped cashews if desired. Leave some cookies plain or sprinkle them with additional confectioners' sugar if desired. Let iced cookies stand until set. Store in an airtight container.

Icebox Honey
Cookies

ICEBOX HONEY COOKIES

My Grandma Wruble always had a batch of these in the cookie jar and a roll of dough in the refrigerator ready to slice and bake at a moment's notice.

—**KRISTI GLEASON** FLOWER MOUND, TX

PREP: 20 MIN. + CHILLING
BAKE: 15 MIN./BATCH
MAKES: 8 DOZEN

- 1½ cups shortening
- 2 cups packed brown sugar
- 2 eggs
- ½ cup honey
- 1 teaspoon lemon extract
- 4½ cups all-purpose flour
- 2 teaspoons baking soda
- 2 teaspoons baking powder
- 1 teaspoon salt
- 1 teaspoon ground cinnamon

1. In a large bowl, cream shortening and brown sugar until light and fluffy. Add eggs, one at a time, beating well after each addition. Beat in honey and extract. Combine remaining ingredients; gradually add to creamed mixture and mix well.
2. Shape into two 12-in. rolls; wrap each in plastic wrap. Refrigerate 2 hours or until firm.
3. Preheat oven to 325°. Unwrap and cut into ¼-in. slices. Place 1 in. apart on ungreased baking sheets. Bake 12-14 minutes or until golden brown. Remove to wire racks to cool.

SUGAR COOKIES

This is truly an oldie, dating back to a Swedish woman born in 1877. Her daughter, Esther Davis, shared the recipe with me. She came up with the exact measurements, because her mother cooked by feel and taste.

—**HELEN WALLIS** VANCOUVER, WA

PREP: 30 MIN. • **BAKE:** 10 MIN./BATCH
MAKES: 5 DOZEN

- ½ cup butter, softened
- ½ cup shortening
- 1 cup sugar
- 1 egg
- 1 teaspoon vanilla extract
- 2¼ cups all-purpose flour
- ½ teaspoon baking powder
- ½ teaspoon baking soda
  Additional sugar

1. Preheat oven to 350°. In a large bowl, cream butter, shortening and sugar until light and fluffy. Add egg and vanilla; mix well. Combine flour, baking powder and baking soda; gradually add to creamed mixture.
2. Shape into 1-in. balls. Roll in sugar. Place on greased baking sheet; flatten with a glass. Bake 10-12 minutes or until set. Remove to wire racks to cool completely.

COOKIE NOTES

LEMON OATMEAL SUGAR COOKIES

We like this recipe because it's a tasty twist on traditional sugar cookies. Let the kids help—they'll have fun rolling the dough into balls and flattening them!

—SUSAN MARSHALL

COLORADO SPRINGS, CO

PREP: 30 MIN. + CHILLING
BAKE: 10 MIN./BATCH
MAKES: 6 DOZEN

- 1 **cup butter, softened**
- 2 **cups sugar**
- 2 **eggs**
- 2 **teaspoons grated lemon peel**
- 3 **tablespoons lemon juice**
- 2¾ **cups all-purpose flour**
- 1 **cup quick-cooking oats**
- 2 **teaspoons baking powder**
- ¼ **teaspoon salt**
  Additional sugar

1. In a large bowl, cream butter and sugar until light and fluffy. Beat in eggs, lemon peel and lemon juice. In another bowl, whisk flour, oats, baking powder and salt; gradually beat into creamed mixture. Refrigerate, covered, 2 hours or until firm enough to shape.

2. Preheat oven to 375°. Shape level tablespoons of dough into balls; place 2 in. apart on parchment paper-lined baking sheets. Coat bottom of a glass with cooking spray, then dip in sugar. Press cookies with bottom of glass to flatten, redipping in sugar as needed.

3. Bake 6-8 minutes or until edges are light brown. Remove from pans to wire racks to cool.

COCONUT RASPBERRY COOKIES

With their yummy raspberry centers, these delectable cookies will disappear from your table fast. My mother used to make them—they were always my favorite, and now my family enjoys them just as much. Store the cooled cookies in a sealed container to keep them soft.

—CHERYL GIROUX AMHERSTBURG, ON

PREP: 30 MIN. • **BAKE:** 10 MIN./BATCH
MAKES: 2½ DOZEN

- ½ cup shortening
- ½ cup packed brown sugar
- 6 tablespoons sugar
- 1 egg
- ¼ cup water
- ½ teaspoon almond extract
- 1½ cups plus 2 tablespoons all-purpose flour
- ½ teaspoon salt
- ½ teaspoon baking soda
- 1 cup flaked coconut
- ⅓ cup seedless raspberry jam

1. In a large bowl, cream shortening and sugars until light and fluffy. Beat in the egg, water and extract. Combine the flour, salt and baking soda; gradually add to creamed mixture and mix well. Stir in coconut (dough will be sticky).

2. Set aside ⅔ cup dough; roll remaining dough into 1-in. balls. Using the end of a wooden spoon handle, make a ⅜-in.-deep indentation in the center of each ball. Fill each with ½ teaspoon jam. Cover jam with a teaspoonful of reserved dough; seal and reshape into a ball. Repeat.

3. Place 2 in. apart on ungreased baking sheets. Bake at 375° for 10-12 minutes or until lightly browned. Remove to wire racks to cool.

JOE FROGGERS

Big, soft and scrumptious, these make a great snack. The classic recipe has a warm blend of spices that seems to be more pronounced the second day.
—*TASTE OF HOME* TEST KITCHEN

PREP: 15 MIN. + CHILLING
BAKE: 15 MIN./BATCH
MAKES: 1½ DOZEN

- ½ cup shortening
- 1 cup packed brown sugar
- 1 cup molasses
- ⅓ cup hot water
- 2 tablespoons rum or 1 teaspoon rum extract
- 3½ cups all-purpose flour
- 1½ teaspoons salt
- 1½ teaspoons ground ginger
- 1 teaspoon baking soda
- ½ teaspoon ground cloves
- ½ teaspoon ground nutmeg
- ¼ teaspoon ground allspice
  Sugar

1. In a large bowl, cream shortening and brown sugar until light and fluffy. In a small bowl, whisk molasses, hot water and rum. In another bowl, whisk the flour, salt and spices; add to creamed mixture alternately with molasses mixture, beating after each addition. Refrigerate, covered, 4 hours or until easy to handle.

2. Preheat oven to 375°. Shape dough into 1½-in. balls and place 3 in. apart on greased baking sheets. Flatten to ½-in. thickness with bottom of a custard cup dipped in sugar.

3. Bake 12-14 minutes or until lightly browned. Cool on pans 2 minutes. Remove cookies to wire racks to cool completely. Store in airtight containers.

VIENNESE COOKIES

I love to cook and bake—when I worked at a medical clinic, I became known as the Cookie Lady. A Swedish friend gave me this recipe. I often make three or four batches so I have plenty to share and send.
—**BEVERLY STIRRAT** MISSION, BC

PREP: 35 MIN. + CHILLING
BAKE: 10 MIN./BATCH + COOLING
MAKES: ABOUT 3 DOZEN

- 1¼ cups butter, softened
- ⅔ cup sugar
- 2¼ cups all-purpose flour
- 1⅔ cups ground almonds
- 1 cup apricot preserves
- 2 cups (12 ounces) semisweet chocolate chips
- 2 tablespoons shortening

1. In a large bowl, cream butter and sugar until light and fluffy. Combine flour and ground almonds; gradually add to creamed mixture and mix well. Cover and refrigerate 1 hour.

2. Preheat oven to 350°. On a lightly floured surface, roll dough to ¼-in. thickness. Cut with a floured 2¼-in. round cookie cutter. Place 2 in. apart on ungreased baking sheets. Bake 7-9 minutes or until edges are lightly browned. Remove to wire racks to cool completely.

3. Spread preserves on the bottoms of half of the cookies; top with remaining cookies. In a microwave, melt chocolate chips and shortening; stir until smooth. Dip half of each sandwich cookie into chocolate mixture; allow excess to drip off. Place on waxed paper until set. Store in an airtight container.

Viennese Cookies

FOLDED HAZELNUT COOKIES

We first made these cookies when my boys were small, and they would end up covered in flour and with Nutella on their faces. Such good memories!

—**PAULA MARCHESI** LENHARTSVILLE, PA

PREP: 30 MIN. • **BAKE:** 10 MIN./BATCH
MAKES: ABOUT 2 DOZEN

- 1 **tablespoon finely chopped hazelnuts**
- 1 **tablespoon sugar**
- 1½ **cups all-purpose flour**
- ½ **cup confectioners' sugar**
- ¼ **cup cornstarch**
- ¾ **cup cold butter, cubed**
- 2 **tablespoons Nutella**
- 1 **egg, lightly beaten**

1. Preheat oven to 350°. In a small bowl, mix hazelnuts and sugar. In a large bowl, whisk flour, confectioners' sugar and cornstarch. Cut in butter until crumbly. Transfer to a clean work surface. Knead gently until mixture forms a smooth dough, about 2 minutes (dough will be crumbly but will come together).

2. Divide dough in half. On a lightly floured surface, roll each portion to ⅛-in. thickness. Cut with a floured 2-in. round cookie cutter. Place ¼ teaspoon Nutella in center. Fold dough partially in half, just enough to cover filling.

3. Place 1 in. apart on greased baking sheets. Brush with beaten egg; sprinkle with hazelnut mixture. Bake 10-12 minutes or until bottoms are light brown. Remove from pans to wire racks to cool.

CHOCOLATE PRETZELS

A rich chocolate coating decorated with a pretty vanilla drizzle makes these homemade cocoa-flavored pretzel cookies hard to resist. My grandkids and I love making them together, and we love eating them just as much!

—KAREN NEMETH CALGARY, AB

PREP: 30 MIN.
BAKE: 10 MIN./BATCH + COOLING
MAKES: 4 DOZEN

- ½ **cup butter, softened**
- ½ **cup shortening**
- 1 **cup confectioners' sugar**
- 1 **egg**
- 1½ **teaspoons vanilla extract**
- 2¼ **cups all-purpose flour**
- ½ **cup baking cocoa**
- 1 **teaspoon salt**

GLAZE
- 3 **ounces semisweet chocolate, chopped**
- 3 **tablespoons butter**
- 3 **cups confectioners' sugar**
- 5 **tablespoons water**
- ½ **cup white baking chips**

1. Preheat oven to 375°. In a large bowl, cream butter, shortening and confectioners' sugar until light and fluffy. Beat in egg and vanilla. Combine flour, cocoa and salt; gradually add to creamed mixture and mix well.

2. Shape into 1-in. balls. Roll each into a 7-in. rope. On greased baking sheets, form each rope into a pretzel shape, placing 2 in. apart.

3. Bake 8-9 minutes or until firm. Cool 1 minute before removing to wire racks to cool completely.

4. For glaze, in a microwave-safe bowl, melt chocolate and butter; stir until smooth. Stir in confectioners' sugar and water until smooth. Dip pretzels in glaze; allow excess to drip off.

5. Place on waxed paper. Melt white chips; drizzle over half of the pretzels. Let stand until completely set. Store in an airtight container.

DRIZZLING MADE EASY

Here's a quick, simple trick for drizzling melted chocolate over treats: After melting, put the chocolate in a resealable plastic bag and cut a small hole in one corner. While slowly moving back and forth over cookies, gently squeeze out the chocolate. The results will be picture-perfect!

SCALLOPED MOCHA COOKIES

I tore this recipe out of a magazine many years ago, and it's one of my most requested. I love these cookies because they have the "four C's": coffee, chocolate, cinnamon and crunch. The coarse sugar on top adds a little glitz.

—LORAINE MEYER BEND, OR

PREP: 30 MIN. + CHILLING
BAKE: 10 MIN./BATCH • **MAKES:** 5 DOZEN

- ⅔ **cup butter, softened**
- 1 **cup sugar**
- 1 **egg**
- 2 **ounces unsweetened chocolate, melted and cooled**
- ½ **teaspoon vanilla extract**
- 1¾ **cups all-purpose flour**
- 1 **tablespoon instant coffee granules**
- ¼ **teaspoon ground cinnamon**
- ⅛ **teaspoon salt**
  Coarse sugar or edible glitter

1. In a small bowl, cream butter and sugar until light and fluffy. Beat in the egg, chocolate and vanilla. Combine the flour, coffee granules, cinnamon and salt; gradually add to creamed mixture.

2. Shape dough into a disk; wrap in plastic wrap. Refrigerate 1 hour or until easy to handle.

3. Preheat oven to 350°. On a floured surface, roll out dough to ¼-in. thickness. Cut with a floured 2¼-in. scalloped cookie cutter. Place 2 in. apart on ungreased baking sheets. Sprinkle with coarse sugar or edible glitter.

4. Bake 8-9 minutes or until set. Remove to wire racks.

NOTE *Edible glitter is available from Wilton Industries. Call 800-794-5866 or visit* wilton.com.

GIANT MONSTER COOKIES

Who can resist a gigantic cookie full of chocolate chips, M&M's and peanut butter? If your appetite isn't quite monster size, scoop the dough by heaping tablespoonfuls instead.

—JUDY FREDENBERG MISSOULA, MT

PREP: 20 MIN. + CHILLING
BAKE: 15 MIN./BATCH
MAKES: ABOUT 2½ DOZEN

- **2 cups creamy peanut butter**
- **⅔ cup butter, softened**
- **1⅓ cups sugar**
- **1⅓ cups packed brown sugar**
- **4 eggs**
- **2½ teaspoons baking soda**
- **1 teaspoon vanilla extract**
- **1 teaspoon light corn syrup**
- **6 cups old-fashioned oats**
- **1 cup semisweet chocolate chips**
- **1 cup milk chocolate M&M's**

1. In a large bowl, cream peanut butter, butter, sugar and brown sugar until light and fluffy, about 4 minutes. Beat in eggs, baking soda, vanilla and corn syrup. Add oats and mix well. Stir in chocolate chips and M&M's. Cover and refrigerate 1 hour.

2. Preheat oven to 350°. Drop by ¼ cupfuls 3 in. apart onto ungreased baking sheets. Bake 14-18 minutes or until edges are lightly browned. Cool 5 minutes before removing from pans to wire racks to cool completely. Store in an airtight container.

Vanilla Crescents

> These cookies are especially cozy at Christmastime but are truly wonderful all year long. Try them dipped into milk or coffee.
> —CARA MCDONALD WINTER PARK, CO

VANILLA CRESCENTS

PREP: 20 MIN. • **BAKE:** 10 MIN./BATCH
MAKES: 4 DOZEN

- 1 cup unsalted butter, softened
- ½ cup sugar
- 1 teaspoon vanilla extract
- ⅛ teaspoon almond extract
- 2 cups all-purpose flour
- 1¼ cups ground almonds
- ½ teaspoon salt
  Confectioners' sugar

1. Preheat oven to 350°. In a large bowl, cream butter and sugar until light and fluffy. Beat in extracts. In another bowl, whisk flour, almonds and salt; gradually beat into creamed mixture.
2. Divide dough into four portions. On a lightly floured surface, roll each portion into a 24-in. rope. Cut crosswise into twelve 2-in. logs; shape each into a crescent. Place 1½ in. apart on ungreased baking sheets.
3. Bake 10-12 minutes or until set. Cool on pans 2 minutes before removing to a wire rack. Dust warm cookies with confectioners' sugar.

OATMEAL CHIP COOKIES

My mom liked to experiment with different flavorings in traditional recipes to come up with unexpected combinations. Molasses and chocolate chips make these stand out from ordinary oatmeal cookies.
—**SUSAN HENRY** BULLHEAD CITY, AZ

PREP: 20 MIN. • **BAKE:** 10 MIN.
MAKES: ABOUT 1½ DOZEN

- ½ cup shortening
- 1 cup sugar
- 1 tablespoon molasses
- 1 egg
- 1 teaspoon vanilla extract
- 1 cup all-purpose flour
- 1 cup quick-cooking oats
- 1 teaspoon baking soda
- 1 teaspoon ground cinnamon
- ½ teaspoon salt
- 1 cup (6 ounces) semisweet chocolate chips

1. Preheat oven to 350°. In a large bowl, cream shortening and sugar until light and fluffy. Beat in molasses, egg and vanilla. Combine flour, oats, baking soda, cinnamon and salt; gradually add to creamed mixture and mix well. Stir in chocolate chips.
2. Roll into 1½-in. balls. Place 2 in. apart on greased baking sheets. Bake 8-10 minutes or until golden brown. Cool 5 minutes before removing from pans to wire racks.

Chocolate-Dipped
Orange Spritz

Classics With a Twist

CHOCOLATE-DIPPED ORANGE SPRITZ

Tired of your usual spritz cookies? Add a burst of tangy citrus with this two-tone variation. They're scrumptious and look extra special on a platter.

—ALISSA STEHR GAU-ODERNHEIM, GERMANY

PREP: 20 MIN. • **BAKE:** 10 MIN./BATCH + COOLING
MAKES: 4 DOZEN

- ¾ cup butter, softened
- 1 cup sugar
- 1 egg
- 2 tablespoons orange juice
- 4 teaspoons grated orange peel
- 2¾ cups all-purpose flour
- 1 teaspoon baking powder
- ¼ teaspoon salt
- ½ cup ground walnuts
- 1 cup (6 ounces) semisweet chocolate chips
- 1 tablespoon shortening

1. Preheat oven to 350°. In a bowl, cream butter and sugar until light and fluffy. Gradually beat in egg, orange juice and peel. In another bowl, whisk flour, baking powder and salt; gradually add to creamed mixture, mixing well.

2. Using a cookie press fitted with a bar disk, press long strips of dough onto ungreased baking sheets; cut ends to release from disk. Cut each strip into 3-in. lengths (no need to separate them).

3. Bake 8-10 minutes or until set (do not brown). Re-cut cookies if necessary. Remove from pans to wire racks to cool completely.

4. Place the walnuts in a shallow bowl. In a microwave, melt chocolate chips and shortening; stir until smooth. Dip each cookie halfway in chocolate; allow excess to drip off. Sprinkle with walnuts. Place on waxed paper; let stand until set.

add to creamed mixture and mix well. Stir in nuts.

2. Shape tablespoonfuls of dough into 1-in. balls. Place 2 in. apart on ungreased baking sheets. Bake 12-14 minutes or until set.

3. In a small bowl, combine cinnamon and remaining confectioners' sugar. Roll warm cookies in sugar mixture; cool on wire racks. Store in an airtight container.

BUTTERY LACE COOKIES

I worked with a group of engineers for over 30 years, and these cookies were a favorite of theirs. They go so well with a steaming cup of coffee or tea.

—LILLIE DUHON PORT NECHES, TX

PREP: 10 MIN.
BAKE: 10 MIN./BATCH + COOLING
MAKES: ABOUT 9 DOZEN

- 2 **cups quick-cooking oats**
- 2 **cups sugar**
- 3 **tablespoons all-purpose flour**
- ½ **teaspoon baking powder**
- 2 **eggs**
- 1 **teaspoon vanilla extract**
- 1 **teaspoon lemon extract**
- ¼ **teaspoon almond extract**
- 1 **cup butter, melted**
- 1 **cup chopped pecans**

1. Preheat oven to 350°. In a large bowl, combine oats, sugar, flour and baking powder. Add eggs, one at a time, beating well after each addition. Beat in extracts. Stir in butter and pecans.

2. Drop by teaspoonfuls 3 in. apart onto lightly greased foil-lined baking sheets. Bake 10-12 minutes or until lacy and golden brown. Cool completely on baking sheets before carefully removing to wire racks.

CHOCOLATE MEXICAN WEDDING CAKES

Cinnamon adds warmth to this twist on a traditional Mexican treat. Sometimes I add mini chocolate chips to the dough and, after baking, dip the cooled cookies in melted almond bark.

—JOANNE VALKEMA FREEPORT, IL

PREP: 20 MIN. • **BAKE:** 15 MIN./BATCH
MAKES: ABOUT 3½ DOZEN

- 1 **cup butter, softened**
- 1¾ **cups confectioners' sugar, divided**
- 1 **teaspoon vanilla extract**
- 1½ **cups all-purpose flour**
- ¼ **cup cornstarch**
- ¼ **cup baking cocoa**
- ½ **teaspoon salt**
- 1¼ **cups finely chopped pecans or almonds**
- ½ **teaspoon ground cinnamon**

1. Preheat oven to 325°. In a large bowl, cream the butter and 1 cup confectioners' sugar until light and fluffy. Beat in vanilla. Combine flour, cornstarch, cocoa and salt; gradually

NORWEGIAN CHOCOLATE CHIP COOKIES

My best friend, Amber, taught me how to make these treats, which are a mash-up of cinnamon sugar cookies and chocolate chip cookies. A pizza cutter is the best tool for slicing the baked cookies efficiently.
—**BONNIE BRIEN** SURPRISE, AZ

PREP: 25 MIN. • **BAKE:** 15 MIN./BATCH
MAKES: 5 DOZEN

- 1 **cup butter, softened**
- 1⅓ **cups plus 3 tablespoons sugar, divided**
- 2 **eggs**
- 1 **teaspoon vanilla extract**
- 3 **cups all-purpose flour**
- 1 **teaspoon baking powder**
- 1 **cup miniature semisweet chocolate chips**
- ¾ **teaspoon ground cinnamon**

1. Preheat oven to 350°. In a large bowl, cream the butter and 1⅓ cups sugar until light and fluffy. Beat in eggs and vanilla. In another bowl, whisk flour and baking powder; gradually beat into creamed mixture. Stir in the chocolate chips.

2. Divide dough into four portions. On a lightly floured surface, roll each portion into a 15-in. rope. Place two ropes 4 in. apart on a parchment paper-lined 15x10x1-in. baking pan; flatten each with a fork to ¼-in. thickness. Mix cinnamon and remaining sugar; sprinkle about 2 teaspoons mixture over each rectangle. Repeat with remaining ropes.

3. Bake 15-17 minutes or until the edges are light brown. Cool on pans 2 minutes; immediately cut each rectangle into 1-in. slices. Remove to wire racks to cool.

TRUFFLE-FILLED COOKIE TARTS

PREP: 65 MIN. + COOLING
COOK: 20 MIN. + CHILLING
MAKES: 2½ DOZEN

- ½ **cup butter, softened**
- ½ **cup sugar**
- ½ **cup packed brown sugar**
- 1 **egg**
- 1 **teaspoon vanilla extract**
- 1½ **cups all-purpose flour**
- ⅓ **cup baking cocoa**
- ¼ **teaspoon baking soda**

FILLING

- 2 **cups (12 ounces) semisweet chocolate chips**
- ⅔ **cup heavy whipping cream**
- ¼ **cup butter, cubed**
- 2 **egg yolks**
  Chocolate sprinkles

1. Preheat oven to 400°. In a large bowl, beat butter and sugars until blended. Beat in egg and vanilla. In another bowl, whisk flour, cocoa and baking soda; gradually beat into creamed mixture.

2. Shape level tablespoons of dough into 2½-in.-wide patties. Press onto bottoms and up the sides of greased mini-muffin cups.

3. Bake 8-10 minutes or until set. Immediately press a deep indentation in center of each with the end of a wooden spoon handle. Cool in pans 5 minutes. Remove to wire racks to cool completely.

4. For filling, in a small heavy saucepan, combine chocolate chips, cream and butter; cook and stir over medium heat until smooth. Remove from heat.

5. In a small bowl, whisk a small amount of hot mixture into egg yolks; return all to pan, whisking constantly. Cook over low heat 15-17 minutes or until mixture is thickened and a thermometer reads at least 160°, stirring constantly. Do not allow to boil. Immediately transfer filling to a bowl; cool 20 minutes, stirring occasionally.

6. Spoon 1 tablespoon filling into each crust. Top with sprinkles. Refrigerate until cold, about 1 hour.

For many years, it has been one of my Christmas traditions to make chocolate truffles. I came up with this recipe as a way to put truffles in the center of a large fudgy cookie. My friends and family are so happy whenever I whip up a batch.
—**PATRICIA HARMON** BADEN, PA

Truffle-Filled
Cookie Tarts

MOLASSES CRACKLE COOKIES

You can treat yourself to one or two of these crackle cookies without any guilt. Most molasses cookies are loaded with butter and have way too much sugar, but mine are just right!

—JEAN ECOS HARTLAND, WI

PREP: 20 MIN. + CHILLING
BAKE: 10 MIN./BATCH
MAKES: 2½ DOZEN

- ⅔ **cup sugar**
- ¼ **cup canola oil**
- 1 **egg**
- ⅓ **cup molasses**
- 2 **cups white whole wheat flour**
- 1½ **teaspoons baking soda**
- 1 **teaspoon ground cinnamon**
- ½ **teaspoon salt**
- ¼ **teaspoon ground ginger**
- ¼ **teaspoon ground cloves**
- 1 **tablespoon confectioners' sugar**

1. In a small bowl, beat sugar and oil until blended. Beat in egg and molasses. Combine the flour, baking soda, cinnamon, salt, ginger and cloves; gradually add to sugar mixture and mix well. Cover and refrigerate at least 2 hours.

2. Preheat oven to 350°. Shape dough into 1-in. balls; roll in confectioners' sugar. Place 2 in. apart on baking sheets coated with cooking spray; flatten slightly. Bake 7-9 minutes or until set. Remove to wire racks to cool.

THICK SUGAR COOKIES

Thicker than most homemade ones, these sugar cookies are like the kind you might find at a good bakery. My children often request these for their birthdays and are always happy to help add the decorations.
—**HEATHER BIEDLER** MARTINSBURG, WV

PREP: 25 MIN. + CHILLING
BAKE: 10 MIN./BATCH + COOLING
MAKES: ABOUT 3 DOZEN

- 1   **cup butter, softened**
- 1   **cup sugar**
- 2   **eggs**
- 3   **egg yolks**
- 1½ **teaspoons vanilla extract**
- ¾ **teaspoon almond extract**
- 3½ **cups all-purpose flour**
- 1½ **teaspoons baking powder**
- ¼ **teaspoon salt**

FROSTING
- 4   **cups confectioners' sugar**
- ½   **cup butter, softened**
- ½   **cup shortening**
- 1   **teaspoon vanilla extract**
- ½   **teaspoon almond extract**
- 2   **to 3 tablespoons 2% milk**
     Assorted colored nonpareils, optional

1. In a large bowl, cream butter and sugar until light and fluffy. Beat in eggs, egg yolks and extracts. In another bowl, whisk flour, baking powder and salt; gradually beat into creamed mixture. Shape into a disk; wrap in plastic wrap. Refrigerate 1 hour or until firm enough to roll.

2. Preheat oven to 375°. On a lightly floured surface, roll dough to ½-in. thickness. Cut with a floured 2-in. cookie cutter. Place 1 in. apart on ungreased baking sheets.

3. Bake 10-12 minutes or until edges begin to brown. Cool on the pans 5 minutes. Remove to wire racks to cool completely.

4. For frosting, in a large bowl, beat confectioners' sugar, butter, shortening, extracts and enough milk to reach desired consistency. Spread over cookies. If desired, sprinkle with nonpareils.

TRIPLE-CHOCOLATE BROWNIE COOKIES

Our family of chocolate lovers gets triply excited when these brownie-textured cookies come out of the oven.

—LINDA ROBINSON NEW BRAUNFELS, TX

PREP: 25 MIN. + CHILLING
BAKE: 10 MIN./BATCH + COOLING
MAKES: 6 DOZEN

- 4 **ounces unsweetened chocolate, chopped**
- ¾ **cup butter, cubed**
- 4 **eggs**
- 2 **cups sugar**
- 1½ **cups all-purpose flour**
- ½ **cup baking cocoa**
- 2 **teaspoons baking powder**
- ½ **teaspoon salt**
- 2 **cups (12 ounces) semisweet chocolate chips, divided**
- 2 **teaspoons shortening**

1. In a microwave, melt chocolate and butter; stir until smooth. Cool slightly. In a large bowl, beat eggs and sugar. Stir in chocolate mixture. Combine the flour, cocoa, baking powder and salt; gradually add to chocolate mixture and mix well. Stir in 1½ cups chocolate chips. Cover and refrigerate 2 hours or until easy to handle.

2. Preheat oven to 350°. Drop by tablespoonfuls 2 in. apart onto greased baking sheets. Bake 7-9 minutes or until edges are set and tops are slightly cracked. Cool 2 minutes before removing from pans to wire racks to cool completely.

3. In a microwave, melt remaining chips and shortening; stir until smooth. Drizzle over cookies. Let stand 30 minutes or until chocolate is set. Store in an airtight container.

LIME SHORTBREAD WITH DRIED CHERRIES

This sweet-tart cookie also works with dried cranberries and orange zest, if you want to switch things up. I freeze the dough for up to a month ahead of time.

—ABIGAIL BOSTWICK TOMAHAWK, WI

PREP: 25 MIN. + CHILLING
BAKE: 10 MIN./BATCH
MAKES: ABOUT 4½ DOZEN

- 1 **cup butter, softened**
- ¾ **cup confectioners' sugar**
- 1 **tablespoon grated lime peel**
- 2 **teaspoons vanilla extract**
- ½ **teaspoon almond extract**
- 2 **cups all-purpose flour**
- ¼ **teaspoon baking powder**
- ⅛ **teaspoon salt**
- ½ **cup chopped dried cherries**

1. In a large bowl, cream butter and confectioners' sugar until blended. Beat in lime peel and extracts. In another bowl, mix flour, baking powder and salt; gradually beat into creamed mixture. Stir in cherries.

2. Divide dough in half; shape each into a 7-in.-long roll. Wrap in plastic wrap; refrigerate 3-4 hours or until firm.

3. Preheat oven to 350°. Unwrap and cut dough crosswise into ¼-in. slices. Place 2 in. apart on ungreased baking sheets. Bake 9-11 minutes or until edges are golden brown. Remove from pans to wire racks to cool.

FREEZE OPTION *Place wrapped logs in resealable plastic freezer bag; freeze. To use, unwrap frozen logs and cut into slices. If necessary, let dough stand a few minutes at room temperature before cutting. Bake as directed.*

Lime Shortbread
with Dried Cherries

TESTING BAKING POWDER

Wondering if your baking powder is still effective? Other than checking the expiration date, you can place 1 teaspoon baking powder in a cup and add ⅓ cup hot tap water. If the mixture bubbles, your baking powder is still good.

RED VELVET WHOOPIE PIES

Everyone gets a kick out of this fun take on the popular cake. If you're short on time, take a shortcut and use ready-made cream cheese frosting for the filling.

—JUDI DEXHEIMER STURGEON BAY, WI

PREP: 40 MIN.
BAKE: 10 MIN./BATCH + COOLING
MAKES: 2 DOZEN

- ¾ **cup butter, softened**
- 1 **cup sugar**
- 2 **eggs**
- ½ **cup sour cream**
- 1 **tablespoon red food coloring**
- 1½ **teaspoons white vinegar**
- 1 **teaspoon clear vanilla extract**
- 2¼ **cups all-purpose flour**
- ¼ **cup baking cocoa**
- 2 **teaspoons baking powder**
- ½ **teaspoon salt**
- ¼ **teaspoon baking soda**
- 2 **ounces semisweet chocolate, melted and cooled**

FILLING

- 1 **package (8 ounces) cream cheese, softened**
- ½ **cup butter, softened**
- 2½ **cups confectioners' sugar**
- 2 **teaspoons clear vanilla extract**

TOPPINGS

- **White baking chips, melted**
- **Finely chopped pecans**

1. Preheat oven to 375°. In a large bowl, cream butter and sugar until light and fluffy. Beat in eggs, sour cream, food coloring, vinegar and vanilla. In another bowl, whisk flour, cocoa, baking powder, salt and baking soda; gradually beat into creamed mixture. Stir in the cooled chocolate.

2. Drop dough by tablespoonfuls 2 in. apart onto parchment paper-lined baking sheets. Bake 8-10 minutes or until edges are set. Cool on pans 2 minutes. Remove to wire racks to cool completely.

3. For filling, in a large bowl, beat cream cheese and butter until fluffy. Beat in confectioners' sugar and vanilla until smooth. Spread the filling on bottom of half of the cookies; cover with remaining cookies.

4. Drizzle with melted baking chips; sprinkle with pecans. Refrigerate until serving.

FREEZE OPTION *Freeze cookies in freezer containers. To use, thaw cookies in covered containers. Fill and decorate as directed.*

CHOCOLATE CHAI SNICKERDOODLES

I used to think snickerdoodles could never be improved—that is, until I added some chocolate. While they're baking, the aromas of chocolate mixed with warming spices reminds me of a cup of hot chai tea.
—**KATHERINE WOLLGAST** FLORISSANT, MO

PREP: 30 MIN. • **BAKE:** 10 MIN./BATCH
MAKES: ABOUT 3 DOZEN

- 2¼ **cups sugar**
- 1 **teaspoon ground ginger**
- 1 **teaspoon ground cardamom**
- 1 **teaspoon ground cinnamon**
- ½ **teaspoon ground allspice**
- ¼ **teaspoon white pepper**
- 1 **cup butter, softened**
- 2 **eggs**
- 2 **teaspoons vanilla extract**
- 2¼ **cups all-purpose flour**
- ½ **cup baking cocoa**
- 2 **teaspoons cream of tartar**
- 1½ **teaspoons baking powder**
- ½ **teaspoon salt**

1. Preheat oven to 350°. In a large bowl, combine the first six ingredients. Remove ½ cup sugar mixture to a shallow dish.

2. Add butter to remaining sugar mixture; beat until light and fluffy. Beat in eggs and vanilla. In another bowl, whisk flour, baking cocoa, cream of tartar, baking powder and salt; gradually beat into creamed mixture.

3. Shape dough into 1½-in. balls. Roll in reserved sugar mixture; place 2 in. apart on ungreased baking sheets. Flatten slightly with bottom of a glass. Bake 10-12 minutes or until edges are firm. Remove to wire racks to cool.

COOKIE NOTES

_____   _____
_____   _____
_____   _____
_____   _____
_____   _____
_____   _____
_____   _____
_____   _____

_____

_____

_____

_____

_____

_____

_____

_____

_____

_____

_____

_____

_____

_____

_____

_____

_____

_____

_____

_____

_____

_____

_____

_____

_____

_____

_____

_____

_____

_____

CHOCOLATE ALMOND CRESCENTS

If you like chocolate-covered almonds, you're in for a real treat. These buttery, crumbly cookies make a thoughtful gift.

—**VICKI RAATZ** WATERLOO, WI

PREP: 20 MIN. + CHILLING
BAKE: 10 MIN./BATCH + COOLING
MAKES: 6 DOZEN

- 1¼ **cups butter, softened**
- ⅔ **cup sugar**
- 2 **cups finely chopped almonds**
- 1½ **teaspoons vanilla extract**
- 2 **cups all-purpose flour**
- ½ **cup baking cocoa**
- ⅛ **teaspoon salt**
- 1¼ **cups semisweet chocolate chips, melted**
- 1 **to 2 tablespoons confectioners' sugar**
  Flaked coconut, optional

1. In a large bowl, cream the butter and sugar until light and fluffy. Beat in almonds and vanilla. In another bowl, whisk flour, cocoa and salt; gradually beat into creamed mixture. Refrigerate, covered, 2 hours or until firm enough to shape.

2. Preheat oven to 350°. Shape 2 teaspoons of dough into 2-in.-long logs. Form each into a crescent. Place 2 in. apart on ungreased baking sheets. Bake 10-12 minutes or until set. Remove from pans to wire racks to cool completely.

3. Dip cookies halfway into melted chocolate, allowing excess to drip off. Place on waxed paper. If desired, sprinkle with coconut. Let stand until set. Cover dipped sides of cookies with waxed paper; dust undipped sides with confectioners' sugar. Store between pieces of waxed paper in airtight containers.

Chocolate
Almond Crescents

HAZELNUT CHOCOLATE CHIP PIZZELLE

I've experimented with different pizzelle recipes, but this is definitely a winner. My dad likes to help make them so that we don't run out!

—AIMEE MCCULLEN YOUNGWOOD, PA

PREP: 15 MIN. • **COOK:** 5 MIN./BATCH
MAKES: 3 DOZEN

- 4 **eggs**
- 1 **cup sugar**
- ¾ **cup butter, melted**
- 2 **cups all-purpose flour**
- ½ **cup finely chopped hazelnuts, toasted**
- ½ **cup miniature semisweet chocolate chips**

1. In a large bowl, beat the eggs, sugar and butter until smooth. Gradually add flour and mix well. Fold in hazelnuts and chocolate chips.

2. Bake in a preheated pizzelle iron according to manufacturer's directions until golden brown. Remove to wire racks to cool. Store in an airtight container.

CHOCOLATE-DIPPED ALMOND MACAROONS

My mother taught my daughter how to make these chocolaty macaroons. When my daughter was 10 years old, she entered a batch in the county fair and won a ribbon.
—**TRACI BOOE** VEEDERSBURG, IN

PREP: 40 MIN.
BAKE: 10 MIN./BATCH + COOLING
MAKES: 6 DOZEN

- 3 **egg whites**
  Dash salt
- 1½ **cups confectioners' sugar**
- 2½ **cups unblanched almonds, finely ground**

CHOCOLATE BUTTERCREAM

- 7 **tablespoons sugar**
- 7 **tablespoons water**
- 4 **egg yolks, lightly beaten**
- ⅔ **cup unsalted butter, softened**
- 1 **tablespoon baking cocoa**

CHOCOLATE DIP

- 9 **ounces semisweet chocolate, chopped and melted**

1. Place egg whites in a small bowl; let stand at room temperature for 30 minutes. Line baking sheets with parchment paper.

2. Preheat oven to 350°. Add salt to the egg whites; beat on medium speed until soft peaks form. Gradually add the confectioners' sugar, 1 tablespoon at a time, beating on high until stiff glossy peaks form and sugar is dissolved. Fold in almonds.

3. Drop by rounded teaspoonfuls 2 in. apart onto prepared baking sheets. Bake 8-12 minutes or until firm to the touch. Cool 5 minutes before removing to wire racks.

4. For buttercream, combine sugar and water in a small heavy saucepan. Bring to a boil; cook over medium-high heat until sugar is dissolved. Remove from heat. Whisk a small amount of hot mixture into egg yolks; return all to pan, stirring constantly. Cook 2 minutes or until mixture is thickened and reaches 160°, stirring constantly. Remove from heat. Cool to room temperature.

5. In a small bowl, beat butter until fluffy, about 5 minutes. Gradually beat in cooked sugar mixture. Beat in cocoa until smooth. If necessary, refrigerate until buttercream reaches spreading consistency.

6. Spread buttercream over bottom of each cooled cookie. Refrigerate until firm, about 15 minutes. Dip bottom of each cookie in melted chocolate, allowing excess to drip off. Place on waxed paper; let stand until set. Store in an airtight container in the refrigerator.

HOMEMADE MACAROON KISSES

These tempting cookies are sure to delight fans of both coconut and chocolate. The combination is simply irresistible.

—LEE ROBERTS RACINE, WI

PREP: 45 MIN. + CHILLING
BAKE: 10 MIN./BATCH + COOLING
MAKES: 4 DOZEN

- ⅓ **cup butter, softened**
- 1 **package (3 ounces) cream cheese, softened**
- ¾ **cup sugar**
- 1 **egg yolk**
- 2 **teaspoons almond extract**
- 1½ **cups all-purpose flour**
- 2 **teaspoons baking powder**
- ½ **teaspoon salt**
- 5 **cups flaked coconut, divided**
- 48 **milk chocolate kisses**
  Coarse sugar

1. In a large bowl, cream the butter, cream cheese and sugar until light and fluffy. Beat in egg yolk and extract. Combine the flour, baking powder and salt; gradually add to creamed mixture and mix well. Stir in 3 cups coconut. Cover and refrigerate for 1 hour or until dough is easy to handle.

2. Preheat oven to 350°. Shape into 1-in. balls and roll in the remaining coconut. Place 2 in. apart on ungreased baking sheets.

3. Bake 10-12 minutes or until lightly browned. Immediately press a chocolate kiss into the center of each cookie; sprinkle with coarse sugar. Cool on pan 2-3 minutes or until chocolate is softened. Remove to wire racks to cool completely.

WASHBOARD COOKIES

These cookies were the treats we would enjoy when we went on family shopping trips many years ago. By the time we got to our destination, they'd be gone!

—JOHN ROULSTON STEPHENVILLE, TX

PREP: 20 MIN. • **BAKE:** 15 MIN.
MAKES: 3½ DOZEN

- ½ **cup butter, softened**
- 1 **cup packed dark brown sugar**
- 1 **egg**
- 1 **tablespoon water**
- 1 **teaspoon vanilla extract**
- 1¾ **cups all-purpose flour**
- ½ **teaspoon baking soda**
  Sugar

1. Preheat oven to 325°. In a small bowl, cream butter and brown sugar until light and fluffy. Beat in egg, water and vanilla. Combine flour and baking soda; add to the creamed mixture and mix well.

2. Shape into 1-in. balls. Place on greased baking sheets; flatten with a fork that has been dipped in water. Sprinkle with sugar.

3. Bake 15-20 minutes or until edges begin to brown. Cool on wire racks.

CORNMEAL LIME COOKIES

Want to add something a little different to your Christmas cookie platter this year? Unique cornmeal cookies with a tart lime glaze will steal the show.

—WENDY RUSCH TREGO, WI

PREP: 45 MIN. + FREEZING
BAKE: 12 MIN./BATCH
MAKES: 8 DOZEN

- 1 **cup butter, softened**
- ½ **cup sugar**
- ½ **cup packed brown sugar**
- 1 **egg**
- ¼ **cup lime juice**
- 4½ **teaspoons grated lime peel**
- 2 **cups all-purpose flour**
- 1 **cup yellow cornmeal**

GLAZE

- 2 **cups confectioners' sugar**
- 3 **tablespoons lime juice**
  Holiday sprinkles

1. In a large bowl, cream butter and sugars until light and fluffy. Beat in egg, lime juice and peel. Combine flour and cornmeal; gradually add to creamed mixture and mix well.

2. Shape into two 12-in. rolls; wrap each in plastic wrap. Refrigerate 30 minutes. Shape each roll into a square-shaped log. Freeze 1 hour or until firm.

3. Preheat oven to 350°. Unwrap logs and cut into ⅜-in. slices. Place 1 in. apart on parchment paper-lined baking sheets. Bake 11-14 minutes or until set. Remove to wire racks to cool completely.

4. Combine confectioners' sugar and lime juice; spread over cookies. Decorate with sprinkles. Let stand until set.

OATMEAL SURPRISE COOKIES

Chocolate-covered raisins and pumpkin pie spice turn these oatmeal cookies into fantastic gourmet snacks! Tuck one into your child's lunch for a little special surprise they'll love.

—REBECCA CLARK WARRIOR, AL

PREP: 20 MIN. • **BAKE:** 15 MIN./BATCH
MAKES: 3 DOZEN

- 1 cup butter, softened
- ¾ cup packed brown sugar
- ½ cup sugar
- 2 eggs
- 1½ cups all-purpose flour
- 1 teaspoon baking soda
- 1 teaspoon pumpkin pie spice
- 2¾ cups quick-cooking oats
- 1½ cups chocolate-covered raisins

1. Preheat oven to 350°. In a large bowl, cream butter and sugars until light and fluffy. Beat in eggs. Combine flour, baking soda and pumpkin pie spice; gradually add to creamed mixture and mix well. Stir in oats and raisins.

2. Drop by tablespoonfuls 2 in. apart onto greased baking sheets. Flatten slightly. Bake 13-15 minutes or until golden brown. Cool 5 minutes before removing to wire racks. Store in an airtight container.

EARL GREY TEA COOKIES

These biscuitlike Earl Grey-flavored cookies are a wonderful alternative to bring to a holiday cookie swap.

—VERONICA CALLAGHAN

GLASTONBURY, CT

PREP: 25 MIN. + COOLING
BAKE: 10 MIN./BATCH + COOLING
MAKES: 3 DOZEN

- 1 **individual Earl Grey tea bag**
- ⅓ **cup boiling water**
- ¼ **cup butter, softened**
- ½ **cup sugar**
- 1 **egg**
- 2 **cups all-purpose flour**
- 1 **teaspoon ground cinnamon, divided**
- ¼ **teaspoon ground cardamom**
- ¼ **teaspoon salt**
- 2 **tablespoons confectioners' sugar**

1. Place tea bag in a 1-cup glass measuring cup. Add boiling water; steep 3-5 minutes. Discard tea bag. Cool completely.

2. Preheat oven to 400°. In a small bowl, cream butter and sugar until light and fluffy. Beat in egg and cooled tea. In another bowl, whisk flour, ½ teaspoon cinnamon, cardamom and salt; gradually beat into creamed mixture.

3. Shape level tablespoons of dough into balls; place 2 in. apart on ungreased baking sheets. Flatten slightly with bottom of a glass.

4. Bake 6-8 minutes or until light brown. Remove to wire racks to cool completely. Mix confectioners' sugar and remaining cinnamon. Dust cookies with cinnamon mixture.

CRANBERRY ORANGE RUGALACH

These buttery cookies get a hint of cranberry and a splash of orange, then a drizzle of chocolate. The result is really quite heavenly!

—GINGER SULLIVAN CUTLER BAY, FL

PREP: 30 MIN. + CHILLING
BAKE: 10 MIN./BATCH
MAKES: 4 DOZEN

- 1 cup butter, softened
- 1 package (8 ounces) cream cheese, softened
- ½ cup sugar
- 2 egg yolks
- ½ teaspoon orange extract
- ½ teaspoon vanilla extract
- 2½ cups all-purpose flour
- ¼ teaspoon salt
- 2 packages (5 ounces each) dried cranberries
- 1½ cups golden raisins
- ½ cup orange juice
- 1 egg, beaten
  Melted chocolate, optional

1. In a large bowl, cream butter, cream cheese and sugar until light and fluffy. Beat in egg yolks and extracts. Combine flour and salt; gradually add to creamed mixture and mix well.

2. Divide dough into four portions. Shape each into a ball, then flatten into a disk. Wrap each in plastic wrap; refrigerate 2 hours or until firm.

3. Preheat oven to 350°. Place cranberries, raisins and juice in a food processor; cover and process until finely chopped. On a lightly floured surface, roll each portion of dough into a 12-in. circle; spread each with ½ cup cranberry mixture. Cut each circle into 12 wedges.

4. Roll up wedges from wide end and place point side down 1 in. apart on greased baking sheets; brush with egg.

5. Bake 10-12 minutes or until lightly browned. Remove to wire racks to cool. Drizzle with melted chocolate if desired. Store in an airtight container.

Cranberry Orange
Rugalach

TRIPLE-GINGER GINGERSNAPS

Ginger cookies are holiday standbys. I tuck them into clean recycled coffee cans wrapped in decorative paper, then add ribbon or trim for a pretty presentation.

—**JESSICA FOLLEN** WAUNAKEE, WI

PREP: 35 MIN. + CHILLING
BAKE: 10 MIN./BATCH
MAKES: 4 DOZEN

- ⅔ cup butter, softened
- 1 cup packed brown sugar
- ¼ cup molasses
- 1 egg
- 2 teaspoons minced fresh gingerroot
- 1 cup all-purpose flour
- ¾ cup whole wheat flour
- 3 teaspoons ground ginger
- 1½ teaspoons baking soda
- ½ teaspoon fine sea salt or kosher salt
- ½ teaspoon ground nutmeg
- ¼ teaspoon ground cloves
- 3 tablespoons finely chopped crystallized ginger
- ¼ cup sugar
- 1½ teaspoons ground cinnamon

1. In a large bowl, cream butter and brown sugar until light and fluffy. Beat in molasses, egg and fresh ginger.

2. Combine flours, ground ginger, baking soda, salt, nutmeg and cloves; gradually add to creamed mixture and mix well. Stir in crystallized ginger. Cover and refrigerate 1 hour or until easy to handle.

3. Preheat oven to 350°. In a small bowl, combine sugar and cinnamon. Shape dough into 1-in. balls; roll in sugar mixture. Place 3 in. apart on parchment paper-lined baking sheets.

4. Bake 10-12 minutes or until set. Cool 2 minutes before removing from pans to wire racks. Store in an airtight container.

FUDGE-FILLED SANDIES

My dream is to own a cookie shop, but until then I'll keep delighting friends and family with my homemade concoctions. These goodies are like pecan sandies with a touch of chocolate.

—JEANETTE RAY LINDENHURST, IL

PREP: 25 MIN.
BAKE: 20 MIN./BATCH + COOLING
MAKES: 4 DOZEN

- 1 **cup butter, softened**
- ¾ **cup confectioners' sugar**
- 1 **teaspoon vanilla extract**
- 2 **cups all-purpose flour**
- 1 **cup finely chopped pecans**
  Additional confectioners' sugar

FILLING

- ¾ **cup semisweet chocolate chips**
- 2 **tablespoons light corn syrup**
- 1 **tablespoon water**
- 1 **tablespoon shortening**

1. Preheat oven to 325°. In a large bowl, cream butter and confectioners' sugar until light and fluffy. Beat in vanilla. Gradually add flour to creamed mixture and mix well. Stir in pecans.
2. Roll into 1-in. balls. Place 1 in. apart on ungreased baking sheets. Using the end of a wooden spoon handle, make an indentation in the center of each. Bake 18-20 minutes or until lightly browned. Roll warm cookies in additional confectioners' sugar; cool on wire racks.
3. In a microwave, melt chocolate chips; stir until smooth. Stir in corn syrup, water and shortening. Spoon or pipe into cooled cookies.

PUMPKIN SEED CRANBERRY BISCOTTI

A hint of pumpkin seed and almond gives these biscotti a wonderful flavor that's just right for a cool day.

—NANCY RENNER EUGENE, OR

PREP: 30 MIN. • **BAKE:** 35 MIN. + COOLING
MAKES: 2½ DOZEN

- ¾ **cup sugar**
- 2 **eggs**
- ¼ **cup canola oil**
- 1½ **teaspoons vanilla extract**
- ½ **teaspoon almond extract**
- 1¾ **cups all-purpose flour**
- 1 **teaspoon baking powder**
- ½ **teaspoon salt**
- 1 **cup salted pumpkin seeds or pepitas, toasted**
- ½ **cup dried cranberries**

1. Preheat oven to 350°. In a small bowl, beat sugar, eggs, oil and extracts. Combine the flour, baking powder and salt; gradually add to sugar mixture and mix well. Stir in pumpkin seeds and cranberries (dough will be sticky).
2. Divide dough in half; place on a baking sheet coated with cooking spray. With lightly floured hands, shape each portion into a 12x2-in. rectangle. Bake 25-30 minutes or until golden brown.
3. Carefully remove to wire racks; cool 10 minutes. Transfer to a cutting board; cut diagonally with a serrated knife into ¾-in. slices. Place cut side down on ungreased baking sheets.
4. Bake 5 minutes or until firm. Turn and bake 5-10 minutes longer or until lightly browned. Remove to wire racks to cool. Store in an airtight container.

3. Cut a small hole in the corner of a pastry or plastic bag; insert #3 star pastry tip. Fill bag with meringue. Pipe 2-in. circles or shapes 2 in. apart onto prepared baking sheets. If desired, sprinkle with pearl or coarse sugar.

4. Bake 20-25 minutes or until set and dry. Turn oven off; leave meringues in oven for 1 hour. Store in an airtight container.

BUTTER BALL CHIFFONS

The combination of lemon pudding and toffee candy bars sets these crisp cookies apart. Keep the ingredients on hand for when you need a snack fast.

—MYLA HARVEY STANTON, MI

START TO FINISH: 30 MIN.
MAKES: 5 DOZEN

- 1 **cup butter, softened**
- ¼ **cup confectioners' sugar**
- 1 **package (3.4 ounces) instant lemon pudding mix**
- 2 **teaspoons water**
- 1 **teaspoon vanilla extract**
- 2 **cups all-purpose flour**
- 1 **cup chopped pecans or walnuts**
- 2 **Heath candy bars (1.4 ounces each), chopped**

1. Preheat oven to 325°. In a small bowl, cream butter and confectioners' sugar until light and fluffy. Beat in pudding mix, water and vanilla. Gradually add flour. Stir in nuts and chopped candy bars.

2. Roll into 1-in. balls. Place 2 in. apart on ungreased baking sheets. Bake 12-15 minutes or until lightly browned. Cool 3 minutes before removing to wire racks.

NOTE *This recipe does not use eggs.*

MERINGUE DROPS

These pretty pastel cookies are a fun way to brighten a springtime luncheon, baby shower or any special occasion. If you don't have time to pipe the meringue, simply spoon it into 2-inch circles. Replace the vanilla with a different extract to change up the flavor.

—TASTE OF HOME TEST KITCHEN

PREP: 25 MIN. • **BAKE:** 20 MIN. + COOLING
MAKES: ABOUT 2 DOZEN

- 3 **egg whites**
- ½ **teaspoon vanilla extract**
- ¼ **teaspoon cream of tartar**
  Food coloring, optional
- ¾ **cup sugar**
  White pearl or coarse sugar, optional

1. Place egg whites in a large bowl; let stand at room temperature for 30 minutes. Line baking sheets with parchment paper.

2. Preheat oven to 300°. Add vanilla, cream of tartar and, if desired, food coloring to egg whites; beat on medium speed until soft peaks form. Gradually beat in sugar, 1 tablespoon at a time, on high until stiff peaks form.

SALTED CASHEW & CARAMEL CHEWS

Nothing says welcome home like warm, gooey cookies fresh from the oven with a cold glass of milk. You don't need a plate—just grab and go!

—PAULA MARCHESI LENHARTSVILLE, PA

PREP: 25 MIN.
BAKE: 10 MIN./BATCH + COOLING
MAKES: ABOUT 3 DOZEN

- ¾ cup unsalted butter, softened
- 1½ cups packed brown sugar
- 2 eggs
- ¼ cup hot caramel ice cream topping
- 1 teaspoon vanilla extract
- 2½ cups all-purpose flour
- ¾ teaspoon baking soda
- ¼ teaspoon salt
- 2 cups (12 ounces) semisweet chocolate chips, divided
- ¾ cup plus ½ cup lightly salted cashew pieces, divided

1. Preheat oven to 350°. In a large bowl, cream butter and brown sugar until light and fluffy. Gradually beat in eggs, caramel topping and vanilla. In another bowl, whisk flour, baking soda and salt; gradually beat into creamed mixture. Stir in 1⅓ cups chocolate chips and ¾ cup cashews.

2. Drop dough by rounded tablespoonfuls 2 in. apart onto parchment paper-lined baking sheets. Bake 10-12 minutes or until edges are firm. Cool on pans 5 minutes. Remove to wire racks to cool completely.

3. In a microwave, melt remaining chocolate chips; stir until smooth. Drizzle over cookies; sprinkle with remaining cashews. Let stand until set.

CHIPOTLE CRACKLE COOKIES

I bake these special cookies for the holidays, birthdays and more! The chipotle chili pepper gives them a little zing. The dough is sometimes sticky, so I dip my hands in confectioners' sugar for easier handling.
—**GLORIA BRADLEY** NAPERVILLE, IL

PREP: 25 MIN. + CHILLING
BAKE: 10 MIN./BATCH
MAKES: 2½ DOZEN

- 2 eggs
- 1 cup sugar
- ¼ cup canola oil
- 2 teaspoons vanilla extract
- 2 ounces unsweetened chocolate, melted and cooled
- 1 cup all-purpose flour
- 1 tablespoon toasted wheat germ
- ¾ teaspoon baking powder
- ¼ teaspoon salt
- ⅛ teaspoon ground chipotle pepper
- ¼ cup miniature semisweet chocolate chips
- ⅓ cup confectioners' sugar

1. In a large bowl, beat eggs, sugar, oil and vanilla until combined. Add melted chocolate. Combine flour, wheat germ, baking powder, salt and chipotle pepper. Gradually add to egg mixture and mix well. Fold in chocolate chips. Cover and refrigerate for 2 hours.
2. Preheat oven to 350°. Place confectioners' sugar in a small bowl. Shape dough into 1-in. balls; roll in confectioners' sugar. Place 2 in. apart on baking sheets coated with cooking spray. Bake 8-10 minutes or until set. Remove to wire racks to cool.

SECRET KISS COOKIES

Here's a recipe that's sealed with a kiss!
—**KAREN OWEN** RISING SUN, IN

PREP: 25 MIN. • **BAKE:** 15 MIN./BATCH
MAKES: 2½ DOZEN

- 1 cup butter, softened
- ½ cup sugar
- 1 teaspoon vanilla extract
- 2 cups all-purpose flour
- 1 cup finely chopped walnuts
- 30 milk chocolate kisses
- 1⅓ cups confectioners' sugar, divided
- 2 tablespoons baking cocoa

1. In a large bowl, cream butter, sugar and vanilla until light and fluffy. Gradually add flour and mix well. Fold in walnuts. Refrigerate dough 2-3 hours or until firm.
2. Preheat oven to 375°. Shape into 1-in. balls. Flatten balls and place a chocolate kiss in the center of each; pinch dough together around kiss. Place 2 in. apart on ungreased baking sheets.
3. Bake 12 minutes or until set but not browned. Cool 1 minute; remove from pans to wire racks.
4. Sift together ⅔ cup confectioners' sugar and cocoa. While cookies are still warm, roll half in cocoa mixture and half in remaining confectioners' sugar. Cool completely. Store in an airtight container.

Giant Dinosaur
Cookies

·Cute Creations·

GIANT DINOSAUR COOKIES

It's fun to cut out these prehistoric shapes and decorate them so they each have their own personality.

—ROBIN WERNER BRUSH PRAIRIE, WA

PREP: 30 MIN. • **BAKE:** 10 MIN.
MAKES: ABOUT 2 DOZEN 4-INCH COOKIES OR 1 DOZEN 8-INCH COOKIES

 1 **cup butter, softened**
 1 **cup sugar**
 1 **egg**
 1 **teaspoon vanilla extract**
 3 **cups all-purpose flour**
 2 **teaspoons baking powder**
    Food coloring, optional
 1 **can (16 ounces) vanilla frosting**
    Miniature or regular semisweet chocolate chips
    Sliced gumdrops or small decorating candies

1. Preheat oven to 400°. In a large bowl, cream butter and sugar. Add egg and vanilla; mix well. Combine flour and baking powder; add to creamed mixture, 1 cup at a time, mixing well after each addition (dough will be very stiff).

2. Divide into two balls; roll each ball directly on an ungreased baking sheet to ¼-in. thickness. Cut cookies with a dinosaur cookie cutter, leaving at least 1 in. between cookies. Remove excess dough and reroll scraps if desired.

3. Bake 7-9 minutes for small cookies and 10-12 minutes for large cookies or until lightly browned around the edges. Cool 1-2 minutes before removing to wire racks.

4. If desired, add food coloring to frosting. Frost cookies. Decorate with chocolate chips for eyes and candies for spots.

CRISPY STAR POPS

These patriotic pops are a hit at our annual Fourth of July party. You can also slip them into cellophane bags, tie on ribbons and give them out as favors.

—COLLEEN STURMA MILWAUKEE, WI

PREP: 30 MIN. • **COOK:** 15 MIN. + COOLING
MAKES: 15 POPS

 8 **cups miniature marshmallows**
 6 **tablespoons butter, cubed**
12 **cups Rice Krispies**
12 **wooden pop sticks**
 1 **cup white baking chips**
 ½ **teaspoon shortening**
    Red, white and blue sprinkles

1. In a Dutch oven, heat marshmallows and butter until melted. Remove from the heat; stir in cereal and mix well. Press into a greased 15x10x1-in. baking pan. Cut with a 3-in. star-shaped cookie cutter. Insert a wooden pop stick into the side of each star; place pops on waxed paper.

2. In a microwave, melt white chips and shortening; stir until smooth. Spread over stars. Decorate with sprinkles.

HALLOWEEN CUTOUT COOKIES

Kids will go batty for these great Halloween cookies—made with, believe it or not, your Christmas cookie cutters.

—TASTE OF HOME TEST KITCHEN

PREP: 30 MIN.
BAKE: 10 MIN./BATCH + COOLING
MAKES: ABOUT 2 DOZEN

- 1 **tube (16½ ounces) refrigerated sugar cookie dough**
- ⅔ **cup all-purpose flour**
- 1 **can (16 ounces) vanilla frosting**
  Green paste food coloring
- 1 **can (16 ounces) chocolate frosting**
  Chocolate wafers, crushed
  Shredded Wheat, M&M's miniature baking bits, miniature semisweet chocolate chips and Fruit Roll-Ups

1. Preheat oven to 350°. Let cookie dough stand at room temperature 5 minutes to soften. In a small bowl, beat cookie dough and flour until combined.

2. On a lightly floured surface, roll dough to ⅛-in. thickness. Cut with a floured 4½-in. Christmas tree-shaped cookie cutter, a 3-in. candy cane-shaped cookie cutter and a 3-in. star-shaped cookie cutter. Cut each star in half. Place 2 in. apart on ungreased baking sheets.

3. Bake 6-8 minutes or until edges are lightly browned. Remove to wire racks to cool completely.

FOR WITCHES *Tint a portion of vanilla frosting green. Frost the bottom two-thirds of a tree cookie green; frost the top third with chocolate frosting. For witches' hats, microwave chocolate wafers for a few seconds to slightly soften as needed. Use a serrated knife to cut a triangle out of one wafer. Cut another wafer in half, forming two hat brims. Place a triangle over chocolate frosting; add a brim. Add Shredded Wheat for hair. Add facial features with baking bits, chocolate chips and cut-up pieces of Fruit Roll-Ups.*

FOR SNAKES *Frost candy cane cookies as desired. Cut Fruit Roll-Ups into triangles; attach to cookies. Add facial features as desired.*

FOR BATS *Frost halved star cookies with chocolate frosting. For ears, microwave chocolate wafers for a few seconds to slightly soften as needed. Use a serrated knife to cut small triangles; attach to cookies. Add facial features as desired.*

Chubby Bunnies

CHUBBY BUNNIES

This soft, adorable cookie bakes up in minutes, and kids will enjoy adding the simple decorations. Sounds like the perfect Easter treat!

—TASTE OF HOME TEST KITCHEN

PREP: 20 MIN.
BAKE: 5 MIN./BATCH + COOLING
MAKES: 16 BUNNIES

- 1 **package yellow cake mix (regular size)**
- 2 **eggs**
- ½ **cup water**
- 15 **drops red food coloring**
- 16 **red gumdrops**
- 32 **miniature semisweet chocolate chips**

1. Preheat oven to 375°. In a large bowl, combine cake mix, eggs and water; beat on low speed 30 seconds. Beat on medium 2 minutes. Reserve 1 cup batter. To the remaining batter, stir in food coloring. Cut a ¼-in. hole in the corner of two food-safe plastic bags; fill one bag with pink batter and one with plain batter.

2. Using pink batter, pipe a 4x2-in. oval ring onto a greased baking sheet for bunny face. Pipe two ovals for ears. Using plain batter, pipe centers for ears and cheeks for face. Pipe additional pink batter to completely fill ears and face. Repeat with remaining batters.

3. Trim off bottom ends of gumdrops; use rounded tops for noses. Add chocolate chips for eyes. Bake 4-6 minutes or until set. Cool 1 minute before removing to wire racks to cool. Store in an airtight container.

STRAWBERRY VALENTINE COOKIES

Start a new Valentine's Day tradition (or just whip 'em up anytime to say "I love you") with these pretty, whimsical cookies. The sweet strawberry flavor is as winning as the shiny chocolate glaze.

—MARNA HEITZ FARLEY, IA

PREP: 50 MIN.
BAKE: 10 MIN./BATCH + COOLING
MAKES: ABOUT 2 DOZEN

- ⅔ cup butter, softened
- ⅔ cup sugar
- 1 egg
- 1 tablespoon lemon juice
- 2 cups all-purpose flour
- ⅓ cup strawberry drink mix
- 2 teaspoons baking powder
- ½ teaspoon salt

GLAZE
- 1 cup (6 ounces) semisweet chocolate chips
- 1 teaspoon shortening

FROSTING
- ⅓ cup butter, softened
- 2 tablespoons strawberry drink mix
- ⅛ teaspoon salt
- 3 cups confectioners' sugar
- 3 to 5 tablespoons 2% milk

1. Preheat oven to 350°. In a small bowl, cream butter and sugar until light and fluffy. Beat in egg and lemon juice. Combine flour, drink mix, baking powder and salt; gradually add to creamed mixture and mix well.

2. On a lightly floured surface, roll out dough to ¼-in. thickness. Cut with a floured 2½- to 3-in. heart-shaped cookie cutter. Place 2 in. apart on ungreased baking sheets. Bake 8-10 minutes or until set and edges begin to brown. Cool 2 minutes before removing to wire racks to cool completely.

3. In a microwave, melt chocolate chips and shortening; stir until smooth. Spread over cookies; let stand until set.

4. In a small bowl, beat butter, drink mix and salt until blended. Gradually beat in confectioners' sugar. Add enough milk to achieve desired consistency. Decorate cookies.

NOTE *This recipe was tested with Nesquik brand drink mix.*

COOKIE NOTES

SPRING GARDEN COOKIE PUZZLE

Ready to roll out the dough and create an edible masterpiece? Kids of all ages will love making this fun-to-paint, even-more-fun-to-eat cookie puzzle. Who says it's bad manners to play with your food?

—*TASTE OF HOME* TEST KITCHEN

PREP: 45 MIN. • **BAKE:** 20 MIN. + COOLING
MAKES: 1 COOKIE PUZZLE

- 1 **tube (16½ ounces) refrigerated sugar cookie dough**
- ½ **cup all-purpose flour**
  Blanched almonds
- 2½ **cups confectioners' sugar**
- 1 **teaspoon vanilla extract**
- 4 **to 5 tablespoons 2% milk**
  Assorted colored sugars and food coloring of your choice

1. Let cookie dough stand at room temperature for 5-10 minutes to soften. In a large bowl, beat cookie dough and flour until blended. On a parchment paper-lined surface, roll dough into a 14x11-in. rectangle. With cookie cutters, cut out puzzle shapes. Slide a baking sheet under the parchment paper and dough. Chill 10 minutes.

2. Meanwhile, preheat oven to 350°. Remove shapes and place on an ungreased baking sheet. Press an almond on its side into the center of each shape for a handle. Bake shapes 7-10 minutes or until edges are golden brown. While still warm, recut shapes with the same cookie cutters to form neat edges. (If cookies cool too quickly, warm in oven to soften.) Remove to wire racks; cool completely.

3. Bake large rectangular puzzle on a parchment paper-lined baking sheet 12-16 minutes or until edges are golden brown. Immediately recut the shapes inside the puzzle to form neat edges. Cool completely on a wire rack.

4. In a small bowl, combine confectioners' sugar, vanilla and enough milk to achieve desired consistency. Frost puzzle and shapes with some of the frosting; decorate with sugars. Tint remaining frosting; pipe as desired. Put shapes back inside puzzle.

GINGERBREAD SKELETONS

A small gingerbread-boy cookie cutter takes on new life with these clever cookies. Give the skeletons some cat friends, too. The more the spookier!

—DORE' MERRICK GRABSKI UTICA, NY

PREP: 15 MIN. + CHILLING
BAKE: 10 MIN./BATCH
MAKES: ABOUT 2 DOZEN

- ⅔ cup shortening
- ½ cup sugar
- ½ cup molasses
- 1 egg
- 3 cups all-purpose flour
- 1 teaspoon baking soda
- 1 teaspoon each ground cinnamon, ginger and cloves
- ½ teaspoon salt
- ½ teaspoon ground nutmeg
  Confectioners' sugar icing

1. In a bowl, cream shortening and sugar. Add molasses and egg; mix well. Combine flour, baking soda, cinnamon, ginger, cloves, salt and nutmeg; gradually add to creamed mixture and mix well. Divide dough in half. Refrigerate at least 2 hours.

2. Preheat oven to 350°. On a lightly floured surface, roll out each portion of dough to ⅛-in. thickness. Cut with a floured 2-in. cookie cutter. Place 2 in. apart on greased baking sheets.

3. Bake 9 minutes or until edges are firm. Remove to wire racks to cool. Decorate as desired.

STAR COOKIES

PREP: 45 MIN.
BAKE: 10 MIN./BATCH + COOLING
MAKES: 22 COOKIES

1½ cups butter, softened
1½ cups sugar
 2 eggs
 3 teaspoons vanilla extract
4½ cups all-purpose flour
 1 teaspoon baking soda
 1 teaspoon cream of tartar
 1 teaspoon salt
   Assorted colors of Jolly Rancher
     hard candies
 1 tablespoon meringue powder
 3 tablespoons plus ½ teaspoon water
2⅔ cups confectioners' sugar
   Assorted colors of paste food
     coloring
   White edible glitter

1. In a large bowl, cream butter and sugar until light and fluffy. Add eggs, one at a time, beating well after each addition. Beat in vanilla. Combine flour, baking soda, cream of tartar and salt; gradually add to creamed mixture. Divide into three portions; cover and refrigerate 30 minutes or until easy to handle.

2. Preheat oven to 350°. Roll out one portion between two pieces of parchment paper to ¼-in. thickness. Cut with a floured 5-in. star-shaped cookie cutter. Cut out centers with a floured 2½-in. star-shaped cookie cutter. Place larger cutouts 2 in. apart on parchment-lined baking sheets. Repeat with remaining dough; reroll small cutouts if desired.

3. Place the same color of hard candies in small resealable plastic bags; crush candies. Sprinkle in center of each cutout. Bake 8-10 minutes or until lightly browned. Cool 2-3 minutes or until candies are set before carefully removing to wire racks.

4. In a small bowl, beat meringue powder and water until soft peaks form. Gradually add the confectioners' sugar. Tint icing to match the selected candies. Decorate cookies with icing; sprinkle with edible glitter.

NOTE *Meringue powder is available from Wilton Industries. Call 800-794-5866 or visit* wilton.com.

These treats are cookies and candies in one pretty package. The melted hard-candy centers look like stained glass surrounded by frosted cutouts.
—*TASTE OF HOME* TEST KITCHEN

BUTTER SNOWMEN COOKIE

These snowmen literally melt in your mouth, but they're almost too cute to eat! If you're looking for an unbeatable bake sale or exchange cookie, this is it.

—KATHLEEN TAUGHER EAST TROY, WI

PREP: 40 MIN. • **BAKE:** 15 MIN./BATCH
MAKES: 1 DOZEN

- 1 **cup butter, softened**
- ½ **cup sugar**
- 1 **tablespoon milk**
- 1 **teaspoon vanilla extract**
- 2¼ **cups all-purpose flour**
  Blue and orange paste food coloring
  Miniature chocolate chips

1. Preheat oven to 325°. In a large bowl, cream butter and sugar until light and fluffy. Add milk and vanilla; mix well. Gradually add flour. Remove ²⁄₃ cup dough to a small bowl; tint blue. Repeat with 1 tablespoon of dough and orange food coloring; set aside.

2. For snowmen, shape white dough into 12 balls, 1¼ in. each; 12 balls, about ½ in. each; and 12 balls, about ⅛ in. each. For bodies, place 1¼-in. balls on two ungreased baking sheets; flatten to ⅜-in. thickness. Place ½-in. balls above bodies for heads; flatten.

3. Shape half of blue dough into 12 triangles. Place triangles above heads for hats; attach ⅛-in. white balls for tassels. Shape orange dough into noses; place on heads. Divide the remaining blue dough into 12 pieces; shape into scarves and position on snowmen. Add chocolate chip eyes and buttons.

4. Bake 13-16 minutes or until set. Cool 2 minutes before carefully removing to wire racks.

COOKIE NOTES

_____   _____
_____   _____
_____   _____
_____   _____
_____   _____
_____   _____

HALLOWEEN PEANUT BUTTER COOKIE POPS

A miniature candy bar is hidden inside these boo-tiful pops. Colored frosting and candy faces make these addictive little snacks the perfect Halloween treat.

—**MARTHA HOOVER** COATESVILLE, PA

PREP: 20 MIN.
BAKE: 15 MIN./BATCH + COOLING
MAKES: 1 DOZEN

- ½ **cup butter, softened**
- ½ **cup creamy peanut butter**
- ½ **cup packed brown sugar**
- ½ **cup sugar**
- 1 **egg**
- 1 **teaspoon vanilla extract**
- 1½ **cups all-purpose flour**
- ½ **teaspoon baking powder**
- ½ **teaspoon baking soda**
- ¼ **teaspoon salt**
- 12 **lollipop sticks**
- 12 **fun-size Snickers or Milky Way candy bars**
  Prepared vanilla frosting
  Food coloring
  Black decorating gel
  Optional decorations: Reese's mini peanut butter cups, candy corn, M&M's minis, mini Chiclets gum and candy eyeballs

1. Preheat oven to 375°. In a small bowl, cream butter, peanut butter and sugars until blended. Beat in egg and vanilla. In a small bowl, whisk flour, baking powder, baking soda and salt; gradually beat into creamed mixture.

2. Insert a lollipop stick into the small end of each candy bar. Divide dough into 12 pieces; wrap one piece around each candy bar. Place 4 in. apart on ungreased baking sheets.

3. Bake 14-16 minutes or until golden brown. Cool on pans 10 minutes; remove to wire racks to cool completely. Tint frosting; frost cookies. Decorate with gel and optional decorations as desired.

SMILING SUGAR COOKIES

I sell these pops for a dollar each at bake sales and then just watch them disappear! The bright, cheery faces always seem to catch kids' eyes.

—BRENDA BAWDON ALPENA, SD

PREP: 30 MIN.
BAKE: 10 MIN. + STANDING
MAKES: ABOUT 2 DOZEN

- ½ **cup butter, softened**
- ½ **cup sugar**
- ½ **cup packed brown sugar**
- 1 **egg**
- ⅓ **cup 2% milk**
- 2 **teaspoons vanilla extract**
- 3 **cups all-purpose flour**
- 2 **teaspoons cream of tartar**
- 1 **teaspoon baking soda**
- ½ **teaspoon salt**
   About 24 wooden pop sticks
- 1 **cup vanilla frosting**

Red, blue and green paste food coloring
Assorted small candies

1. Preheat oven to 375°. In a large bowl, cream butter and sugars until light and fluffy. Beat in egg, milk and vanilla. Combine flour, cream of tartar, baking soda and salt; gradually add to creamed mixture and mix well. Roll dough into 1½-in. balls; insert a wooden pop stick in the center of each.

2. Place 2 in. apart on lightly greased baking sheets; flatten slightly. Bake 8-10 minutes or until lightly browned. Remove to wire racks to cool.

3. Divide frosting among three bowls; tint as desired. Place each color of frosting in a resealable plastic bag; cut a small hole in a corner of bag. Pipe hair and mouths onto cookies; use a dab of frosting to attach small candies for eyes. Let dry at least 30 minutes.

SUGAR DOVES

It's so much fun to spend a cold winter evening decorating these gorgeous goodies. Pretty little sugar doves will get everyone into the holiday spirit.

—PEGGY PRESTON FENTON, IA

PREP: 30 MIN. + CHILLING
BAKE: 10 MIN./BATCH + COOLING
MAKES: 7½ DOZEN

- 1 **cup butter, softened**
- 2 **cups sugar**
- 2 **eggs**
- 2 **tablespoons milk**
- 2 **teaspoons vanilla extract**
- 4¼ **cups all-purpose flour**
- 2 **teaspoons baking powder**
- ¼ **teaspoon salt**

FROSTING
- ½ **cup shortening**
- 3¾ **cups confectioners' sugar**
- 2 **tablespoons milk**
- 1 **teaspoon almond extract**
- ½ **teaspoon vanilla extract**
- 1 **to 2 tablespoons water**
- 4½ **cups sliced almonds**
- 3½ **cups finely chopped walnuts**
    Miniature semisweet chocolate chips

1. In a large bowl, cream butter and sugar until light and fluffy. Add eggs, one at a time, beating well after each addition. Beat in milk and vanilla.

2. In another bowl, whisk flour, baking powder and salt; gradually beat into creamed mixture. Refrigerate, covered, 2 hours or until easy to handle.

3. Preheat oven to 350°. On a lightly floured surface, roll out dough to ⅛-in. thickness. Cut with a 3-in. bird-shaped cookie cutter. Place 1 in. apart on greased baking sheets. Bake 7-9 minutes or until set. Remove from pans to wire racks to cool completely.

4. For frosting, in a small bowl, combine shortening, confectioners' sugar, milk, extracts and enough water to achieve spreading consistency.

5. Frost cookies. Arrange walnuts over the bodies and almonds over the wings and tails. Add chocolate chip eyes.

CHOCOLATE REINDEER

You can enlist little hands to help position the antlers, eyes and noses on these crisp and festive cookies.

—PAT HABIGER SPEARVILLE, KS

PREP: 40 MIN. + CHILLING
BAKE: 10 MIN./BATCH
MAKES: 4 DOZEN

- 1 **cup butter, softened**
- 1½ **cups sugar**
- 3 **eggs**
- 1 **teaspoon vanilla extract**
- 3¼ **cups all-purpose flour**
- ⅓ **cup baking cocoa**
- 2 **teaspoons cream of tartar**
- 1 **teaspoon baking soda**
- ½ **teaspoon salt**
- 96 **miniature pretzels**
- 96 **M&M's miniature baking bits**
- 48 **small red gumdrops**

1. In a large bowl, cream butter and sugar until light and fluffy. Beat in eggs and vanilla. Combine the flour, cocoa, cream of tartar, baking soda and salt; gradually add to creamed mixture and mix well.

2. Divide dough into eight portions; cover and refrigerate for at least 2 hours.

3. Preheat oven to 375°. On a lightly floured surface, roll each portion into a 6-in. circle; cut into six wedges. Place 2 in. apart on ungreased baking sheets. Press in pretzels for antlers, baking bits for eyes and a gumdrop for the nose.

4. Bake 7-9 minutes or until set. Cool 1 minute before removing from pans to wire racks. Store in an airtight container.

COOKIE ANGELS

These easy-to-assemble angels will fly right off your cookie platter!

—*TASTE OF HOME* TEST KITCHEN

PREP: 35 MIN.
BAKE: 10 MIN./BATCH + COOLING
MAKES: 1½ DOZEN

- ⅔ cup butter-flavored shortening
- ¼ cup sugar
- 1 egg
- 1½ cups all-purpose flour
- ½ teaspoon baking powder
- ½ teaspoon salt
- 36 miniature pretzels
- 1 can (16 ounces) vanilla frosting, divided
- ¼ cup confectioners' sugar
  Brown paste food coloring
- 18 yellow Life Savers
- 10 green Life Savers, crushed
  Decorating gels

1. Preheat oven to 350°. In a small bowl, cream shortening and sugar until light and fluffy. Beat in egg. Combine flour, baking powder and salt; gradually add to creamed mixture and mix well. Set aside ½ cup of dough; divide remaining dough into three portions.

2. On a lightly floured surface, roll out each portion into a 6-in. circle; cut each into six wedges. Transfer to ungreased baking sheets.

3. For angel heads, roll teaspoonfuls of reserved dough into 18 balls; lightly press onto pointed end of each wedge. Press a pretzel into each wedge side for the wings.

4. Bake 10-12 minutes or until lightly browned. Remove to wire racks to cool completely.

5. For hair, in a small bowl, beat ¼ cup vanilla frosting and confectioners' sugar until smooth; tint with food coloring. Press dough through a garlic press. Trim strands to desired length; place on heads. For halos, attach yellow Life Savers.

6. Frost gowns with remaining frosting; sprinkle with crushed Life Savers. Use decorating gels to add faces.

COOKIE NOTES

_____   _____
_____   _____
_____   _____
_____   _____
_____   _____

SNOWFLAKE COOKIES

You'll have a twinkle in your eye when you bake up a batch of these winter wonders.

—TASTE OF HOME TEST KITCHEN

PREP: 20 MIN. + CHILLING
BAKE: 10 MIN./BATCH + STANDING
MAKES: ABOUT 3 DOZEN

- 1 **cup butter, softened**
- 1 **cup confectioners' sugar**
- 1 **egg**
- 1 **teaspoon vanilla extract**
- ½ **to 1 teaspoon almond extract**
- 2½ **cups all-purpose flour**
- ½ **teaspoon salt**

ROYAL ICING

- 2 **pounds confectioners' sugar**
- 6 **tablespoons meringue powder**
- ¾ **cup warm water**
  Sky blue gel food coloring
  White edible glitter and superfine sugar
  Ribbon

1. In a large bowl, cream butter and confectioners' sugar until light and fluffy. Beat in egg and extracts. Combine flour and salt; gradually add to the creamed mixture and mix well.

2. Divide dough into fourths. Cover and refrigerate 1-2 hours or until easy to handle.

3. Preheat oven to 375°. On a lightly floured surface, roll out one portion to ⅛-in. thickness. (Refrigerate other portions until ready to use.) Using a variety of sizes of floured snowflake cookie cutters, cut out snowflakes.

4. Carefully place 1 in. apart on ungreased baking sheets. Using small cutters, cut out desired shapes to create designs in some of the snowflakes. Use a toothpick to help remove cutouts. With a plastic straw, poke a hole in the top of each small cookie.

5. Bake medium and large snowflakes 6½ to 7 minutes and small snowflakes 6 minutes or until bottoms are lightly browned. Remove to wire racks to cool. Repeat with remaining dough.

6. For royal icing, in a large bowl, combine confectioners' sugar and meringue powder. Add warm water; beat on low speed 1 minute. Beat on high 4-5 minutes or until stiff peaks form. Tint half blue. Leave remaining icing white; cover and set aside.

7. With blue icing and a round tip, outline half of the cookies; fill in centers with blue icing and let dry completely. With white icing and a round tip, outline each blue cookie and create snowflake designs. Let dry completely.

8. On the remaining cookies, repeat process using white icing on white frosted cookies. Thread a ribbon through the hole in each small snowflake and through the cutout in each medium and large snowflake.

NOTE *Edible glitter and meringue powder are available from Wilton Industries. Call 800-794-5866 or visit wilton.com.*

ALMOND-BUTTER COOKIE BOUQUET

I make these cookie pops often. In the spring, I cut them into flower shapes and insert them into a block of foam fitted inside a basket or bowl. If you like, you can cover the foam with tissue paper or cellophane, then present the bouquet as a great centerpiece or hostess gift.

—**KRISSY FOSSMEYER** HUNTLEY, IL

PREP: 2 HOURS + CHILLING
BAKE: 10 MIN./BATCH + COOLING
MAKES: ABOUT 2½ DOZEN

- 1¼ **cups butter, softened**
- 1¾ **cups confectioners' sugar**
- 2 **ounces almond paste**
- 1 **egg**
- ¼ **cup 2% milk**
- 1 **teaspoon vanilla extract**
- 4 **cups all-purpose flour**
- ½ **teaspoon salt**
- **Wooden skewers or lollipop sticks**

ICING

- 1 **cup confectioners' sugar**
- 4 **teaspoons evaporated milk**
- **Food coloring of your choice**

1. In a large bowl, cream butter and confectioners' sugar until light and fluffy; add almond paste. Beat in egg, milk and vanilla. Combine flour and salt; gradually add to creamed mixture and mix well. Cover and refrigerate 1 hour.

2. Preheat oven to 375°. On a lightly floured surface, roll out dough to ¼-in. thickness. Cut out with floured 3-in. cookie cutters. Place 1 in. apart on ungreased baking sheets. Insert skewers or sticks. Bake 7-8 minutes or until firm. Let stand 2 minutes before removing to wire racks to cool.

3. In a bowl, whisk confectioners' sugar and milk. Divide into small bowls; tint with food coloring. Gently spread icing over cooled cookies. Decorate with other colors of icing if desired.

Chocolate-Dipped
Strawberry Meringue Roses

CHOCOLATE-DIPPED STRAWBERRY MERINGUE ROSES

Enjoy these kid-friendly treats as is, or crush them into a bowl of strawberries and whipped cream. Readers of my blog, *utry.it,* went nuts when I posted that idea!
—**AMY TONG** ANAHEIM, CA

PREP: 25 MIN. • **BAKE:** 40 MIN. + COOLING
MAKES: 3½ DOZEN

- 3 **egg whites**
- ¼ **cup sugar**
- ¼ **cup freeze-dried strawberries**
- 1 **package (3 ounces) strawberry gelatin**
- ½ **teaspoon vanilla extract, optional**
- 1 **cup 60% cacao bittersweet chocolate baking chips, melted**

1. Place egg whites in a large bowl; let stand at room temperature 30 minutes. Preheat oven to 225°.

2. Place sugar and strawberries in a food processor; process until powdery. Add gelatin; pulse to blend.

3. Beat egg whites on medium speed until foamy, adding vanilla if desired. Gradually add gelatin mixture, 1 tablespoon at a time, beating on high after each addition until sugar is dissolved. Continue beating until stiff glossy peaks form.

4. Cut a small hole in the tip of a pastry bag or in a corner of a food-safe plastic bag; insert a #1M star tip. Transfer meringue to bag. Pipe 2-in. roses 1½ in. apart onto parchment paper-lined baking sheets.

5. Bake 40-45 minutes or until set and dry. Turn off oven (do not open oven door); leave meringues in oven 1½ hours. Remove from oven; cool completely on baking sheets.

6. Remove meringues from paper. Dip bottoms in melted chocolate; allow excess to drip off. Place on waxed paper; let stand until set, about 45 minutes. Store in an airtight container at room temperature.

DIPPED BROWNIE POPS

I needed to host a quick fundraiser for a student organization, so I made these brownies on a stick. The kids loved them, and I sold more than 200 in an afternoon! Add crushed graham crackers to the dipped chocolate for a special s'mores version.

—JAMIE FRANKLIN MURTAUGH, ID

PREP: 45 MIN. • **BAKE:** 35 MIN. + COOLING
MAKES: 16 BROWNIE POPS

- 1 **package fudge brownie mix (13x9-in.-pan size)**
- 16 **wooden pop sticks**
- 2/3 **cup semisweet chocolate chips**
- 3 **teaspoons shortening, divided**
- 2/3 **cup white baking chips**
  Assorted sprinkles, chopped pecans and/or miniature marshmallows

1. Line an 8- or 9-in.-square baking pan with foil; grease the foil and set aside. Prepare and bake brownie mix according to package directions for the size baking pan you used. Cool completely on a wire rack.

2. Using foil, lift brownie out of pan; remove foil. Cut brownie into sixteen squares. Gently insert wooden pop stick into the side of each square. Cover and freeze 30 minutes.

3. In a microwave, melt chocolate chips and 1 1/2 teaspoons shortening; stir until smooth. Repeat with white baking chips and remaining shortening.

4. Dip eight brownies halfway into chocolate mixture; allow excess to drip off. Dip remaining brownies halfway into white chip mixture; allow excess to drip off. Sprinkle with toppings of your choice. Place on waxed paper; let stand until set. Place in bags and fasten with twist ties or ribbon if desired.

TOM TURKEYS

With a little prep work by Mom or Dad, these turkeys make a great after-dinner craft project for the kids to tackle.

—*TASTE OF HOME* TEST KITCHEN

PREP: 30 MIN. • **COOK:** 5 MIN. + COOLING
MAKES: 26 TURKEYS

- 1 **package (12 ounces) semisweet chocolate chips**
- 1 **package (11 ounces) candy corn**
- 52 **fudge-striped cookies**
- ¼ **cup butter, cubed**
- 4 **cups miniature marshmallows**
- 6 **cups crisp rice cereal**
- 52 **white confetti sprinkles**

1. In a microwave, melt chocolate chips; stir until smooth. For tails, use a dab of chocolate to attach five candy corns to the chocolate side of half of the cookies in a fan shape; refrigerate until set.

2. In a large saucepan, melt butter. Add the marshmallows; stir over low heat until melted. Stir in cereal. Cool for 10 minutes. With buttered hands, form cereal mixture into 1½-in. balls.

3. Remelt chocolate if necessary. Using chocolate, attach the cereal balls to the chocolate side of the remaining cookies. Position tails perpendicular to the base cookies; attach with chocolate. Refrigerate until set.

4. For feet, cut off white tips from 52 candy corns; discard tips. Attach feet to base cookies with chocolate. Attach one candy corn with chocolate to each cereal ball for heads.

5. With a toothpick dipped in chocolate, attach two confetti sprinkles to each head. Using chocolate, dot each sprinkle to make pupils. Let stand until set. Store in an airtight container.

PERFECTLY MELTED CHOCOLATE

When melting chocolate in the microwave, first grab a microwave-safe bowl. Start by melting the semisweet chocolate chips on high (100% power) for 1 minute; stir. If they aren't quite melted, continue microwaving for 10-20 seconds at a time, stirring until smooth.

_____
_____
_____
_____
_____
_____
_____
_____
_____
_____
_____
_____
_____
_____
_____
_____
_____
_____
_____
_____
_____
_____
_____
_____
_____
_____
_____
_____
_____
_____
_____
_____

GINGERBREAD TEDDY BEARS

These cookies have been a tradition in my family since I was a little girl. They're big, soft and delicious.
—**ELIZABETH MANZANARES** GLOUCESTER, VA

PREP: 40 MIN. + CHILLING
BAKE: 10 MIN./BATCH + COOLING
MAKES: 8 COOKIES

- 1 **cup butter, cubed**
- ⅔ **cup packed brown sugar**
- ⅔ **cup molasses**
- 1 **egg, lightly beaten**
- 1½ **teaspoons vanilla extract**
- 4 **cups all-purpose flour**
- 1½ **teaspoons ground cinnamon**
- 1 **teaspoon ground ginger**
- ¾ **teaspoon baking soda**
- ½ **teaspoon ground cloves**
  Miniature chocolate chips
  Red decorating frosting

1. In a small saucepan, combine butter, brown sugar and molasses. Cook over medium heat until sugar is dissolved. Pour into a large bowl; let stand 10 minutes. Stir in egg and vanilla. Combine flour, cinnamon, ginger, baking soda and cloves; gradually add to butter mixture and mix well. Cover and refrigerate 2 hours or overnight.

2. Preheat oven to 350°. Shape dough into eight balls, 2 in. each; eight balls, 1 in. each; 32 balls, ½ in. each; and 16 balls, ⅜ in. each. Place the 2-in. balls on three foil-lined baking sheets for the body of eight bears; flatten to ½-in. thickness. Position 1-in. balls for heads; flatten to ½-in. thickness. Attach four ½-in. balls to each bear for arms and legs. Attach two ⅜-in. balls for ears. Add chocolate chips for eyes, nose and buttons.

3. Bake 10-12 minutes or until set. Cool 10 minutes before carefully removing to wire racks to cool completely. With frosting, pipe bows on bears.

ELF COOKIES

A simple glaze, colorful candies and sliced almonds for ears turn these sugar cookies into a whole crew of Santa's helpers. Bake a big batch as a classroom treat, or use them to brighten your cookie trays.

—TASTE OF HOME TEST KITCHEN

PREP: 45 MIN. • **BAKE:** 10 MIN.
MAKES: 28 COOKIES

- ½ **tube refrigerated sugar cookie dough, softened**
- ⅓ **cup all-purpose flour**
- 2½ **cups confectioners' sugar**
- 10 **teaspoons water**
- 4 **teaspoons meringue powder**
  Assorted food coloring
  Assorted sprinkles, candies and almond slices

1. Preheat oven to 350°. In a small bowl, beat cookie dough and flour until combined. Roll out on a lightly floured surface to ⅛-in. thickness. Cut with a floured 1¾x3¼-in. diamond cookie cutter. Place 2 in. apart on ungreased baking sheets. Bake 7-9 minutes or until edges are golden brown. Remove to wire racks to cool.

2. In a large bowl, combine confectioners' sugar, water and meringue powder; beat on low speed just until blended. Beat on high 4-5 minutes or until stiff peaks form. Divide icing into portions and tint as desired. Keep unused icing covered at all times with a damp cloth. If necessary, beat again on high speed to restore texture.

3. Frost and decorate cookies as desired with assorted sprinkles and candies; add almonds for ears.

CARAMEL APPLE COOKIES

My little fool-the-eye chocolate chip cookies—no apples included—are always a hit. Top the caramel with your favorite kind of nuts, sprinkles or mini chips.

—TAMMY DANIELS BATAVIA, OH

PREP: 40 MIN.
BAKE: 10 MIN./BATCH + STANDING
MAKES: 4 DOZEN

- ½ cup butter, softened
- ¼ cup confectioners' sugar
- ¼ cup packed brown sugar
- ¼ teaspoon salt
- 1 egg
- ½ teaspoon vanilla extract
- 2 cups all-purpose flour
- ½ cup miniature semisweet chocolate chips
- 48 round toothpicks
- 1 package (11 ounces) Kraft caramel bits
- 2 tablespoons water
- 1 cup finely chopped pecans

1. Preheat oven to 350°. In a large bowl, cream butter, sugars and salt until light and fluffy. Beat in egg and vanilla. Gradually add flour and mix well. Stir in chocolate chips.

2. Shape into 1-in. balls; place 2 in. apart on greased baking sheets. Bake 10-12 minutes or until set. Immediately insert a round toothpick in center of each cookie. Remove to wire racks to cool completely.

3. In a small saucepan, combine caramel bits and water. Cook and stir over medium-low heat until smooth. Holding a cookie by the toothpick, dip cookie in the caramel mixture, turning to coat. Allow excess to drip off. Immediately dip the bottom and sides in pecans.

4. Place on waxed paper. Repeat with remaining cookies, caramel mixture and pecans. Let stand until set.

PIGGY POPS

My mother-in-law and I made these cookie pops for a bake sale. Wrap them in little cellophane bags and tie off with a piece of pink pipe cleaner, then curl the pipe cleaner around a pencil for a squiggly tail.

—LORRI REINHARDT BIG BEND, WI

PREP: 1 HOUR + COOLING
MAKES: 32 POPS

- **16 large pink and/or white marshmallows**
- **1 tablespoon sugar**
- **2 packages (10 to 12 ounces each) white baking chips**
- **2 tablespoons shortening**
- **3 to 4 drops red food coloring, optional**
- **32 double-stuffed Oreo cookies**
- **32 wooden pop sticks**
- **64 miniature semisweet chocolate chips (about 1 tablespoon)**
- **64 M&M's miniature baking bits (about 2 tablespoons)**

1. Cut marshmallows into thirds horizontally; cut the center portion of each into four wedges for ears. Roll cut sides of ears in sugar to prevent sticking together. Set ears and remaining portions aside.
2. In a microwave, melt baking chips and shortening; stir until smooth. Stir in food coloring if desired.

3. Twist apart sandwich cookies. Dip the end of a wooden pop stick into melted baking chip mixture and place on a cookie half; replace cookie top. Repeat. Place pops on waxed paper-lined baking sheets; refrigerate for 10 minutes or until set.
4. Reheat baking chip mixture if necessary; dip a pop in mixture and allow excess to drip off. Return to waxed paper-lined baking sheet. While wet, position a marshmallow slice on the cookie for a snout. Add ears on top edge of cookie; hold for a few seconds or until set. Add chocolate chip eyes. Place two baking bits on snout, securing with a dab of baking chip mixture. Repeat. Let stand until set.

COOKIE NOTES

_____

_____

_____

_____

Unlike the real woodland creatures, these chocolaty hedgehogs happily dwell on snack plates. They're as much fun to make as they are to eat.

—**PAM GOODLET** WASHINGTON ISLAND, WI

HEDGEHOG COOKIES

PREP: 30 MIN.
BAKE: 15 MIN./BATCH + COOLING
MAKES: 16 COOKIES

- ⅓ **cup butter, softened**
- ¼ **cup confectioners' sugar**
- ½ **teaspoon vanilla extract**
- ⅔ **cup all-purpose flour**
- ⅔ **cup ground pecans**
- ⅛ **teaspoon salt**
- ½ **cup 60% cacao bittersweet chocolate baking chips**
- ¼ **cup chocolate sprinkles**

1. Preheat oven to 325°. In a small bowl, cream butter and confectioners' sugar until light and fluffy. Beat in vanilla. Combine flour, pecans and salt; gradually add to creamed mixture and mix well. Shape 1 tablespoon of dough into a ball; pinch the dough to form a face. Repeat. Place 2 in. apart on a greased baking sheet.

2. Bake 12-15 minutes or until lightly browned. Let stand 5 minutes before removing to a wire rack to cool completely.

3. In a microwave, melt chocolate; stir until smooth. Holding a hedgehog cookie by the nose, spoon chocolate over the back (leave face uncovered). Allow excess to drip off. Place on waxed paper; immediately coat the wet chocolate with sprinkles.

4. With a toothpick dipped in chocolate, make two eyes and a dot on the nose. Let stand until set. Store in an airtight container.

CHECK SOFTENED BUTTER

Before creaming butter, check to see if it's soft enough. When softened, you should be able to easily glide a table knife through butter.

SNOW ANGEL COOKIES

Get a little snow at the holidays, no matter where you are. Head to the kitchen and bake a batch of angel cookies dusted with cinnamon, nutmeg and cloves.

—CAROLYN MOSELEY DAYTON, OH

PREP: 40 MIN. + CHILLING
BAKE: 15 MIN./BATCH + COOLING
MAKES: ABOUT 5 DOZEN

- **1 cup butter, softened**
- **1 cup sugar**
- **1½ teaspoons vanilla extract**
- **2 eggs**
- **3½ cups all-purpose flour**
- **1 teaspoon ground cinnamon**
- **½ teaspoon baking powder**
- **½ teaspoon salt**
- **¼ teaspoon ground nutmeg**
- **¼ teaspoon ground cloves**

FROSTING

- **9 cups confectioners' sugar**
- **¾ cup shortening**
- **½ cup lemon juice**
- **4 to 6 tablespoons water**
  Coarse sugar

1. In a large bowl, beat butter, sugar and vanilla until blended. Beat in eggs, one at a time. In another bowl, whisk flour, cinnamon, baking powder, salt, nutmeg and cloves; gradually beat into creamed mixture.

2. Divide dough in half. Shape each into a disk; wrap in plastic wrap. Refrigerate 1 hour or until firm enough to roll.

3. Preheat oven to 350°. On a lightly floured surface, roll each portion of dough to ⅛-in. thickness. Cut with a floured 4-in. angel-shaped cookie cutter. Place 1 in. apart on ungreased baking sheets.

4. Bake 12-14 minutes or until edges begin to brown. Remove from pans to wire racks to cool completely.

5. For frosting, in a large bowl, beat confectioners' sugar, shortening, lemon juice and enough water to reach a spreading consistency. Spread or pipe over cookies; sprinkle with coarse sugar.

CHRISTMAS MICE COOKIES

Add some whimsy to your next gathering with these little cuties that taste like truffles. Every Christmas, we make sure to have enough for friends and neighbors.

—DEBORAH ZABOR FORT ERIE, ON

PREP: 30 MIN. + CHILLING
MAKES: 1½ DOZEN

- ⅔ cup semisweet chocolate chips
- 2 cups chocolate wafer crumbs, divided
- ⅓ cup sour cream
- 36 red nonpareils
- ¼ cup sliced almonds
- 18 pieces black shoestring licorice (2 inches each)

1. In a microwave, melt chocolate chips; stir until smooth. Stir in 1 cup wafer crumbs and sour cream. Refrigerate, covered, 1 hour or until firm enough to shape.

2. Place remaining wafer crumbs in a shallow bowl. For each mouse, roll about 1 tablespoon crumb mixture into a ball; taper one end to resemble a mouse. Roll in wafer crumbs to coat. Attach nonpareils for eyes, sliced almonds for ears and licorice pieces for tails. Store in an airtight container in the refrigerator.

ORANGE SUGAR COOKIES

I make these yummy cookies for special occasions—the ones that don't come out perfectly always go to my delighted family.

—MYRRH WERTZ MILWAUKEE, WI

PREP: 25 MIN. + CHILLING
BAKE: 10 MIN./BATCH + COOLING
MAKES: 2½ DOZEN

- 1 cup butter, softened
- 1 cup sugar
- ½ teaspoon salt
- 1 egg
- 4 teaspoons grated orange peel
- ⅓ cup orange juice
- 1½ teaspoons lemon extract
- 2½ cups all-purpose flour

ICING

- 1 cup confectioners' sugar
- 2 tablespoons 2% milk
- 3 drops orange food coloring, optional

1. In a large bowl, cream butter, sugar and salt until light and fluffy. Beat in egg, orange peel, orange juice and extract. Gradually beat in flour.

2. Divide dough in half. Shape each into a disk; wrap in plastic wrap. Refrigerate 1 hour or until firm enough to roll.

3. Preheat oven to 375°. On a floured surface, roll each portion of dough to ¼-in. thickness. Cut with a floured 2½-in. cookie cutter. Place 1 in. apart on greased baking sheets.

4. Bake 8-10 minutes or until edges are light brown. Remove from pans to wire racks to cool completely.

5. In a small bowl, mix confectioners' sugar, milk and, if desired, food coloring until smooth. Pipe or spread over cookies; let stand until set.

HALLOWEEN PUMPKIN BARS

My family loves the warm pumpkin fragrance that drifts through our kitchen on cool afternoons when I make these. Jack-o'-lantern faces add to the fall fun.
—**KARLA JOHNSON** EAST HELENA, MT

PREP: 30 MIN. • **BAKE:** 20 MIN. + COOLING
MAKES: 35 BARS

- 1½ cups pumpkin pie filling
- 2 cups sugar
- 1 cup canola oil
- 4 eggs
- 1 teaspoon vanilla extract
- 2 cups all-purpose flour
- 2 teaspoons baking powder
- 1 teaspoon baking soda
- ½ teaspoon salt
- 1 cup chopped pecans
- 1 can (16 ounces) cream cheese frosting
  Yellow and red food coloring
- 70 pieces candy corn
- ½ cup milk chocolate chips

1. Preheat oven to 350°. In a large bowl, beat pumpkin, sugar, oil, eggs and vanilla. Combine flour, baking powder, baking soda and salt; gradually add to pumpkin mixture and mix well. Stir in pecans.

2. Pour into a greased 15x10x1-in. baking pan. Bake 20-25 minutes or until a toothpick inserted near the center comes out clean. Cool on a wire rack.

3. Tint frosting orange with yellow and red food coloring. Frost bars; cut into 35 squares. For eyes, place two pieces of candy corn on each bar.

4. In a microwave, melt chocolate chips; stir until smooth. Transfer to a heavy-duty resealable plastic bag; cut a small hole in a corner of the bag. Pipe dots on candy corn for pupils; decorate faces as desired.

WHEN TO CHOP NUTS

If the word "chopped" comes before a recipe ingredient, that means you should chop it before measuring. If the word comes after the ingredient, measure first, then chop.

_____
_____
_____
_____
_____
_____
_____
_____
_____
_____
_____
_____
_____
_____
_____
_____
_____
_____
_____
_____
_____
_____
_____
_____
_____
_____
_____
_____
_____
_____
_____
_____
_____
_____
_____

OWL COOKIES

These funny owl faces are a hoot at my kids' class parties. They're crunchy, munchy and peanut buttery.
—STARRLETTE HOWARD OGDEN, UT

PREP: 35 MIN. + CHILLING • **BAKE:** 15 MIN.
MAKES: 1 DOZEN

- ⅔ **cup butter, softened**
- 1 **cup creamy peanut butter**
- 1 **cup packed brown sugar**
- 1 **egg**
- 1 **teaspoon vanilla extract**
- 1⅓ **cups all-purpose flour**
- 1 **cup quick-cooking oats**
- 1 **teaspoon baking powder**
- ½ **teaspoon salt**
- 1 **ounce unsweetened chocolate, melted**
- 12 **whole cashews**
- 24 **striped chocolate kisses, unwrapped**
- 24 **semisweet chocolate chips**

1. In a bowl, beat butter, peanut butter and brown sugar until blended. Beat in egg and vanilla. In another bowl, mix flour, oats, baking powder and salt; gradually beat into creamed mixture.

2. If necessary, cover and refrigerate dough 1 hour or until firm enough to shape. Divide dough in half; shape one portion into an 8-in.-long roll. Mix melted chocolate into remaining dough. Roll chocolate dough between two sheets of waxed paper into an 8-in. square. Place plain roll on chocolate dough. Wrap chocolate dough around plain dough, pinching together at the seam to seal. Wrap in plastic wrap; refrigerate until firm.

3. Preheat oven to 350°. Unwrap and cut dough crosswise into 24 slices ⅜ in. thick. To make owls, place two slices side by side on an ungreased baking sheet; pinch the top of each slice for ears. Add a cashew beak. Repeat with remaining dough.

4. Bake 12-15 minutes or until set. Cool on pans 5 minutes before removing to wire racks. While cookies are warm, place two kisses on each cookie, pointed side down, for eyes. (Kisses will melt slightly.) Top each kiss with a chocolate chip. Cool.

Owl Cookies

Chewy Honey
Granola Bars

In the Pan

CHEWY HONEY GRANOLA BARS

These snacks have it all: sweetness from the honey, chewiness from the raisins, plus chocolate, cinnamon and a bit of crunch. To save a few for later, wrap individual bars in plastic wrap and place in a resealable freezer bag. When you want a satisfying treat on short notice, just grab one and let it thaw for a few minutes.

—TASHA LEHMAN WILLISTON, VT

PREP: 10 MIN.
BAKE: 15 MIN. + COOLING
MAKES: 20 SERVINGS

- 3 **cups old-fashioned oats**
- 2 **cups unsweetened puffed wheat cereal**
- 1 **cup all-purpose flour**
- ⅓ **cup chopped walnuts**
- ⅓ **cup raisins**
- ⅓ **cup miniature semisweet chocolate chips**
- 1 **teaspoon baking soda**
- 1 **teaspoon ground cinnamon**
- 1 **cup honey**
- ¼ **cup butter, melted**
- 1 **teaspoon vanilla extract**

1. Preheat oven to 350°. In a large bowl, combine the first eight ingredients. In a small bowl, combine honey, butter and vanilla; pour over oat mixture and mix well. (Batter will be sticky.)
2. Press into a 13x9-in. baking pan coated with cooking spray. Bake 14-18 minutes or until set and edges are lightly browned. Cool on a wire rack. Cut into bars.

CHEWY CHOCOLATE-CHERRY BARS

Colorful dried cherries and pistachios join in this new take on seven-layer bars. Want even more options? Substitute cinnamon or chocolate graham cracker crumbs for the plain ones and try pecans or walnuts instead of the pistachios.

—TASTE OF HOME TEST KITCHEN

PREP: 10 MIN. ● **BAKE:** 25 MIN. + COOLING
MAKES: 3 DOZEN

- 1½ **cups graham cracker crumbs**
- ½ **cup butter, melted**
- 1 **can (14 ounces) sweetened condensed milk**
- 1½ **cups dried cherries**
- 1½ **cups semisweet chocolate chips**
- 1 **cup flaked coconut**
- 1 **cup pistachios, chopped**

1. Preheat oven to 350°. In a small bowl, mix cracker crumbs and butter. Press into a greased 13x9-in. baking pan. In a large bowl, mix remaining ingredients until blended; carefully spread over crust.
2. Bake 25-28 minutes or until edges are golden brown. Cool in pan on a wire rack. Cut into bars.

ALMOST A CANDY BAR

Because I love candy bars and marshmallows, this recipe was a cinch to invent. With all the different layers and flavors, these sweet surprises please just about everyone.

—**BARB WYMAN** HANKINSON, ND

PREP: 15 MIN. • **BAKE:** 15 MIN. + CHILLING
MAKES: 3 DOZEN

- 1 **tube (16½ ounces) refrigerated chocolate chip cookie dough**
- 4 **chewy s'mores granola bars, chopped**
- 1 **package (10 to 11 ounces) butterscotch chips**
- 2½ **cups miniature marshmallows**
- 1 **cup chopped walnuts**
- 1½ **cups miniature pretzels**
- 1 **package (10 ounces) peanut butter chips**
- ¾ **cup light corn syrup**
- ¼ **cup butter, cubed**
- 1 **package (11½ ounces) milk chocolate chips**

1. Preheat oven to 350°. Let dough stand at room temperature for 5-10 minutes to soften. In a large bowl, combine dough and granola bars. Press into an ungreased 13x9-in. baking pan. Bake, uncovered, 10-12 minutes or until golden brown.

2. Sprinkle with butterscotch chips and marshmallows. Bake 3-4 minutes longer or until marshmallows begin to brown. Sprinkle with the walnuts; arrange pretzels over the top. In a small saucepan, melt the peanut butter chips, corn syrup and butter; spoon over bars.

3. In a microwave, melt chocolate chips; stir until smooth. Spread or drizzle over bars. Refrigerate 1 hour or until firm before cutting.

CREAM CHEESE SWIRL BROWNIES

I'm a chocolate lover, and these have satisfied my serious sweet tooth many times. No one guesses they're on the light side, because of their wonderfully chewy texture and rich chocolate taste.

—HEIDI JOHNSON WORLAND, WY

PREP: 20 MIN. • **BAKE:** 25 MIN.
MAKES: 1 DOZEN

- 3 **eggs**
- 6 **tablespoons butter, softened**
- 1 **cup sugar, divided**
- 3 **teaspoons vanilla extract**
- ½ **cup all-purpose flour**
- ¼ **cup baking cocoa**
- 1 **package (8 ounces) reduced-fat cream cheese**

1. Preheat oven to 350°. Separate two eggs, putting each white in a separate bowl (discard yolks or save for another use); set aside. In a small bowl, beat butter and ¾ cup sugar until crumbly. Beat in the whole egg, one egg white and vanilla until well combined. Combine flour and cocoa; gradually add to egg mixture until blended. Pour into a 9-in.-square baking pan coated with cooking spray; set aside.

2. In a small bowl, beat cream cheese and remaining sugar until smooth. Beat in the second egg white. Drop by rounded tablespoonfuls over the batter; cut through batter with a knife to swirl.

3. Bake 25-30 minutes or until set and edges pull away from sides of pan. Cool on a wire rack.

Frosted Banana Bars

FROSTED BANANA BARS

I make these moist bars whenever I have ripe bananas on hand, then store them in the freezer to share later at a potluck. With creamy frosting and a big banana boost, this recipe is a guaranteed crowd-pleaser.

—DEBBIE KNIGHT MARION, IA

PREP: 15 MIN. • **BAKE:** 20 MIN. + COOLING
MAKES: 3-4 DOZEN

- ½ cup butter, softened
- 1½ cups sugar
- 2 eggs
- 1 cup (8 ounces) sour cream
- 1 teaspoon vanilla extract
- 2 cups all-purpose flour
- 1 teaspoon baking soda
- ¼ teaspoon salt
- 2 medium ripe bananas, mashed (about 1 cup)

FROSTING

- 1 package (8 ounces) cream cheese, softened
- ½ cup butter, softened
- 2 teaspoons vanilla extract
- 3¾ to 4 cups confectioners' sugar

1. Preheat oven to 350°. In a large bowl, cream butter and sugar until light and fluffy. Add eggs, sour cream and vanilla. Combine flour, baking soda and salt; gradually add to creamed mixture. Stir in bananas.

2. Spread into a greased 15x10x1-in. baking pan. Bake 20-25 minutes or until a toothpick inserted near the center comes out clean (do not overbake). Cool.

3. For frosting, in a large bowl, beat cream cheese, butter and vanilla until fluffy. Gradually beat in enough confectioners' sugar to achieve desired consistency. Frost bars. Store in the refrigerator.

HONEY-PECAN SQUARES

When we left Texas to head north, a neighbor gave me pecans from his trees. I'm happy to send these squares back to him.
—**LORRAINE CALAND** SHUNIAH, ON

PREP: 15 MIN. • **BAKE:** 30 MIN.
MAKES: 2 DOZEN

- 1 **cup unsalted butter, softened**
- ¾ **cup packed dark brown sugar**
- ½ **teaspoon salt**
- 3 **cups all-purpose flour**

FILLING
- ½ **cup unsalted butter, cubed**
- ½ **cup packed dark brown sugar**
- ⅓ **cup honey**
- 2 **tablespoons sugar**
- 2 **tablespoons heavy whipping cream**
- ¼ **teaspoon salt**
- 2 **cups chopped pecans, toasted**
- ½ **teaspoon maple flavoring or vanilla extract**

1. Preheat oven to 350°. Line a 13x9-in. baking pan with parchment paper, letting ends extend up sides of pan. In a bowl, cream butter, brown sugar and salt until light and fluffy. Gradually beat in flour. Press into prepared pan. Bake 16-20 minutes or until lightly browned.
2. In a small saucepan, combine first six filling ingredients; bring to a boil. Cook 1 minute. Remove from heat; stir in pecans and maple flavoring. Pour over crust.
3. Bake 10-15 minutes or until bubbly. Cool in pan on a wire rack. Lifting with parchment paper, transfer to a cutting board; cut into bars.
NOTE *To toast nuts, bake in a shallow pan in a 350° oven for 5-10 minutes or cook in a skillet over low heat until lightly browned, stirring occasionally.*

RICH BUTTERSCOTCH BARS

My husband works second shift, so I spend a few nights a week baking just for fun. He takes half my sweets to his co-workers, who can't resist these decadent delights.
—**KATHRYN ROTH** JEFFERSON, WI

PREP: 15 MIN. • **BAKE:** 30 MIN + COOLING
MAKES: 3 DOZEN

- 1 **package (10 to 11 ounces) butterscotch chips**
- ½ **cup butter, cubed**
- 2 **cups graham cracker crumbs (about 32 squares)**
- 1 **package (8 ounces) cream cheese, softened**
- 1 **can (14 ounces) sweetened condensed milk**
- 1 **egg**
- 1 **teaspoon vanilla extract**
- 1 **cup chopped pecans**

1. Preheat oven to 325°. In a microwave, melt chips and butter; stir until smooth. Add cracker crumbs; set aside ⅔ cup. Press the remaining crumb mixture into a greased 13x9-in. baking pan.
2. In a small bowl, beat cream cheese until smooth. Beat in milk, egg and vanilla. Stir in pecans.
3. Pour over crust. Sprinkle with reserved crumb mixture. Bake 30-35 minutes or until a toothpick inserted near the center comes out clean. Cool on a wire rack. Store in the refrigerator.

CHOCOLATE SAUCE BROWNIES

These moist, cakelike brownies are loaded with crunchy nuts and topped with a homemade chocolate frosting. No matter where I serve them, I always get the same reaction: *Mmm!*

—**VICKIE OVERBY** WAHPETON, ND

PREP: 20 MIN. • **BAKE:** 20 MIN.
MAKES: 5 DOZEN

- ½ **cup butter, softened**
- 1 **cup sugar**
- 4 **eggs**
- 1 **can (16 ounces) chocolate syrup**
- 1 **teaspoon vanilla extract**
- 1 **cup plus 1 tablespoon all-purpose flour**
- ½ **teaspoon baking powder**
- 1 **cup chopped pecans or walnuts**

FROSTING

- 1 **cup sugar**
- 6 **tablespoons milk**
- 6 **tablespoons butter**
- ½ **cup semisweet chocolate chips**

1. Preheat oven to 350°. In a bowl, cream the butter and sugar. Add eggs, one at a time, beating well after each addition. Stir in chocolate syrup and vanilla. Combine flour and baking powder; add to creamed mixture and mix well. Stir in nuts.

2. Pour into a greased 15x10x1-in. baking pan. Bake 20-25 minutes or until a toothpick inserted near the center comes out clean. Cool on a wire rack.

3. For frosting, combine sugar, milk and butter in a heavy saucepan. Bring to a boil over medium heat boil 1 minute. Remove from heat. Add chocolate chips; stir or whisk 5 minutes or until smooth. Spread over brownies.

GERMAN CHOCOLATE BROWNIES

Even as a young girl, I was always going through recipe books in search of something new to make. That's how I came across these brownies, a favorite for our family reunions and other get-togethers.

—**KAREN GRIMES** STEPHENS CITY, VA

PREP: 20 MIN. • **BAKE:** 25 MIN. + COOLING
MAKES: 16 BROWNIES

- ½ **cup butter, cubed**
- 4 **ounces German sweet chocolate, coarsely chopped**
- 2 **eggs, lightly beaten**
- ½ **cup sugar**
- 1 **teaspoon vanilla extract**
- 1 **cup all-purpose flour**
- ½ **teaspoon baking powder**
- ¼ **teaspoon salt**

TOPPING

- 2 **tablespoons butter, melted**
- ½ **cup packed brown sugar**
- 1 **cup flaked coconut**
- ½ **cup chopped pecans**
- 2 **tablespoons corn syrup**
- 2 **tablespoons 2% milk**

1. Preheat oven to 350°. In a microwave, melt butter and chocolate; stir until smooth. Cool slightly. In a large bowl, beat eggs and sugar. Stir in vanilla and chocolate mixture. Combine flour, baking powder and salt; gradually add to chocolate mixture.

2. Pour into a greased 9-in.-square baking pan. Bake 18-22 minutes or until a toothpick inserted near the center comes out clean (do not overbake).

3. For topping, combine butter and brown sugar in a large bowl. Add coconut, pecans, corn syrup and milk; mix well. Drop by teaspoonfuls onto warm brownies; spread evenly.

4. Broil 6 in. from heat 2-4 minutes or until top is browned and bubbly. Cool on a wire rack. Cut into bars.

COBBLESTONE BROWNIES

Chocolate and coconut is my family's idea of a great combo, so I stirred coconut extract into brownie batter and added flaked coconut to the cream cheese filling. These fudgy bars are the fabulous result!

—PHYLLIS PERRY VASSAR, KS

PREP: 15 MIN.
BAKE: 45 MIN. + COOLING
MAKES: 3 DOZEN

- 1 **package fudge brownie mix (13x9-inch pan size)**
- ½ **cup canola oil**
- 2 **eggs**
- ½ **teaspoon coconut extract**

FILLING

- 1 **package (8 ounces) cream cheese, softened**
- 2 **eggs**
- 1 **teaspoon coconut extract**
- 1 **teaspoon vanilla extract**
- 3¾ **cups confectioners' sugar**
- 1 **cup flaked coconut**

1. Preheat oven to 350°. In a large bowl, beat brownie mix, oil, eggs and extract on medium speed until blended (batter will be stiff). Set aside 1 cup for topping.
2. Spread the remaining batter into a greased 13x9-in. baking pan. Bake 10-15 minutes or until edges crack.
3. For filling, in a large bowl, beat cream cheese, eggs and extracts until smooth. Gradually add confectioners' sugar and mix well. Fold in coconut; carefully spread over brownies.
4. Drop reserved batter by teaspoonfuls over filling. Bake 45-50 minutes or until a toothpick inserted near center comes out clean (do not overbake). Cool on a wire rack. Store in the refrigerator.

PEANUT BUTTER CAKE BARS

Packed with peanut butter and chocolate chips, these bars are at home anywhere. Adults love them as much as kids do.

—CHARLOTTE ENNIS LAKE ARTHUR, NM

PREP: 15 MIN. • **BAKE:** 45 MIN. + COOLING
MAKES: 2 DOZEN

- ⅔ **cup butter, softened**
- ⅔ **cup peanut butter**
- 1 **cup sugar**
- 1 **cup packed brown sugar**
- 4 **eggs**
- 2 **teaspoons vanilla extract**
- 2 **cups all-purpose flour**
- 2 **teaspoons baking powder**
- ½ **teaspoon salt**
- 1 **package (11½ ounces) milk chocolate chips**

1. Preheat oven to 350°. In a large bowl, cream butter, peanut butter, sugar and brown sugar. Add eggs, one at a time, beating well after each addition. Beat in vanilla. Combine the flour, baking powder and salt; gradually add to creamed mixture. Stir in chocolate chips.
2. Spread into a greased 13x9-in. baking pan. Bake 45-50 minutes or until a toothpick inserted near the center comes out clean. Cool on a wire rack. Cut into bars.

CALGARY NANAIMO BARS

This version may claim roots in Alberta, but the original was said to have been dreamed up in a kitchen in Nanaimo, British Columbia. Either way, they're three delicious layers of Canadian goodness.

—CAROL HILLIER CALGARY, AB

PREP: 25 MIN. + CHILLING
MAKES: 3½ DOZEN

- ¼ **cup sugar**
- ¼ **cup baking cocoa**
- ¾ **cup butter, cubed**
- 2 **eggs, beaten**
- 2 **cups graham cracker crumbs**
- 1 **cup flaked coconut**
- ½ **cup chopped almonds, optional**

FILLING

- 2 **cups confectioners' sugar**
- 2 **tablespoons instant vanilla pudding mix**
- ¼ **cup butter, melted**
- 3 **tablespoons 2% milk**

GLAZE

- 3 **ounces semisweet chocolate, chopped**
- 1 **tablespoon butter**

1. Line an 8-in.-square baking pan with foil, letting ends extend over sides by 1 in. In a large heavy saucepan, combine sugar and cocoa; add butter. Cook and stir over medium-low heat until butter is melted. Whisk a small amount of the hot mixture into eggs. Return all to the pan, whisking constantly. Cook and stir until mixture reaches 160°. Remove from heat.

2. Stir in cracker crumbs, coconut and, if desired, almonds. Press into prepared pan. Refrigerate 30 minutes or until set.

3. For filling, in a small bowl, beat confectioners' sugar, pudding mix, butter and milk until smooth; spread over crust.

4. In a microwave, melt the chocolate and butter; stir until smooth. Spread over top. Refrigerate until set. Using foil, lift bars out of pan. Discard foil; cut into bars.

TRIPLE-LAYER PRETZEL BROWNIES

If you've ever thought about trying a brownie pie with a pretzel crust and peanut butter-chocolate topping, your dreams have come true.

—CATHIE AYERS HILTON, NY

PREP: 30 MIN. • **BAKE:** 35 MIN. + COOLING
MAKES: 2 DOZEN

- 3 **cups crushed pretzels**
- ¾ **cup butter, melted**
- 3 **tablespoons sugar**
- 1 **package fudge brownie mix (13x9-inch pan size)**
- ¾ **cup semisweet chocolate chips**
- ½ **cup creamy peanut butter**

1. Preheat oven to 400°. In a small bowl, combine pretzels, butter and sugar. Press into an ungreased 13x9-in. baking dish. Bake 8 minutes. Cool on a wire rack.

2. Reduce heat to 350°. Prepare brownie mix batter according to the package directions. Pour over prepared crust. Bake 35-40 minutes or until a toothpick inserted near the center comes out with moist crumbs (do not overbake). Cool completely on a wire rack.

3. In a microwave, melt chocolate chips and peanut butter; stir until smooth. Spread over top. Refrigerate 30 minutes or until firm. Cut into bars. Store in an airtight container.

CHOCOLATE TOFFEE DELIGHTS

I combined a good shortbread recipe with some ingredients I had on hand and came up with these wonderful bars, which remind me of my favorite Girl Scout cookies. Yum!
—**SHANNON KOENE** BLACKSBURG, VA

PREP: 15 MIN. • **BAKE:** 30 MIN. + COOLING
MAKES: 3 DOZEN

- 1 **cup butter, softened**
- ½ **cup plus 2 tablespoons sugar, divided**
- ¾ **teaspoon almond extract**
- ½ **teaspoon coconut extract**
- 2 **cups all-purpose flour**
- ¼ **teaspoon salt**
- ¼ **teaspoon baking powder**
- ½ **cup flaked coconut**
- ½ **cup sliced almonds, toasted and cooled**
- 1 **jar (12¼ ounces) caramel ice cream topping**
- ¾ **cup dark chocolate chips**

1. Preheat oven to 350°. In a small bowl, cream butter and ½ cup sugar until light and fluffy. Beat in extracts. Combine flour, salt and baking powder; gradually add to creamed mixture and mix well.

2. Press into a greased 13x9-in. baking pan. Bake 10 minutes. Prick crust with a fork; sprinkle with remaining sugar. Bake 15 minutes longer or until set.

3. Meanwhile, place coconut and almonds in a food processor; cover and process until finely chopped. Transfer to a small bowl; stir in ice cream topping. Spread over crust. Bake 5-10 minutes or until edges are bubbly. Cool on a wire rack.

4. In a microwave, melt chocolate chips; stir until smooth. Drizzle over caramel mixture. Let stand until chocolate is set. Cut into bars. Store in an airtight container.

Coconut Chip
Nut Bars

COCONUT CHIP NUT BARS

PREP: 15 MIN. • **BAKE:** 20 MIN. • **MAKES:** 3 DOZEN

1¾ cups all-purpose flour
¾ cup confectioners' sugar
¼ cup baking cocoa
1¼ cups cold butter, cubed
1 can (14 ounces) sweetened condensed milk
2 cups (12 ounces) semisweet chocolate chips, divided
1 teaspoon vanilla extract
1 cup chopped walnuts
½ cup flaked coconut
½ cup English toffee bits or almond brickle chips

1. Preheat oven to 350°. In a small bowl, combine flour, sugar and cocoa. Cut in butter until mixture resembles coarse crumbs. Press firmly into a greased 13x9-in. baking pan. Bake 10 minutes.

2. Meanwhile, in a small saucepan, combine milk and 1 cup chocolate chips; cook and stir over low heat until smooth and chips are melted. Stir in vanilla.

3. Pour over crust. Sprinkle with walnuts and remaining chocolate chips. Top with coconut and toffee bits. Gently press down into chocolate layer. Bake 18-20 minutes longer or until firm. Cool on a wire rack. Cut into bars.

There's something for everyone here, from coconut and chocolate chips to walnuts and toffee.
—**JUDITH STROHMEYER** ALBRIGHTSVILLE, PA

COCONUT CITRUS BARS

Three kinds of juice and grated peel are the secrets to these amazing bars with loads of citrus in every bite. The unique crust and vibrant orange zing makes them tastier than traditional lemon bars.

—**HEATHER ROTUNDA** ST. CLOUD, MN

PREP: 30 MIN. • **BAKE:** 20 MIN. + COOLING
MAKES: 2 DOZEN

- ¾ cup butter, softened
- ⅓ cup confectioners' sugar
- 1½ cups all-purpose flour
- ½ cup crisp rice cereal
FILLING
- 4 eggs
- 1½ cups sugar
- 1 cup flaked coconut
- ⅓ cup orange juice
- ¼ cup lemon juice
- 2 tablespoons lime juice
- 2 tablespoons all-purpose flour
- 3 teaspoons grated orange peel
- 2 teaspoons grated lemon peel
- 1½ teaspoons grated lime peel
  Confectioners' sugar

1. Preheat oven to 350°. In a small bowl, cream butter and confectioners' sugar until light and fluffy; gradually beat in flour until crumbly. Stir in cereal. Press into a greased 13x9-in. baking pan. Bake 18-22 minutes or until lightly browned.

2. Meanwhile, in a large bowl, beat eggs, sugar, coconut, juices, flour and peels until frothy. Pour over hot crust. Bake 18-22 minutes longer or until lightly browned. Cool on a wire rack. Dust with confectioners' sugar; cut into bars. Store in the refrigerator.

PEANUT BUTTER CRISPY BARS

I needed something quick for a gathering and whipped up this yummy creation.

—**GAIL ANDERSON** JEFFERSON, WI

PREP: 15 MIN. • **BAKE:** 15 MIN. + COOLING
MAKES: 3 DOZEN

- 1 tube (16½ ounces) refrigerated peanut butter cookie dough
- 4 cups miniature marshmallows
- 2 cups (12 ounces) semisweet chocolate chips
- ½ cup creamy peanut butter
- ¼ cup butter, cubed
- 2 cups crisp rice cereal
- ½ cup salted peanuts

1. Preheat oven to 350°. Press cookie dough into an ungreased 13x9-in. baking pan. Bake 10-14 minutes or until edges are lightly browned and center is set. Sprinkle with marshmallows; bake 4-5 minutes or just until marshmallows are puffed. Cool 5 minutes.

2. Meanwhile, in a small saucepan, combine chocolate chips, peanut butter and butter. Cook and stir until chocolate is melted and mixture is smooth. Remove from heat; stir in cereal and peanuts. Drop by spoonfuls over top; gently spread over the marshmallows. Cool and cut into bars.

ULTIMATE DOUBLE CHOCOLATE BROWNIES

We live in the city, but just a block away we can see cattle grazing in a grassy green pasture, a sight that I never tire of. As someone who grew up in the country, I love home-style recipes like these brownies.

—CAROL PREWETT CHEYENNE, WY

PREP: 15 MIN. • **BAKE:** 35 MIN.
MAKES: 3 DOZEN

- ¾ cup baking cocoa
- ½ teaspoon baking soda
- ⅔ cup butter, melted, divided
- ½ cup boiling water
- 2 cups sugar
- 2 eggs
- 1⅓ cups all-purpose flour
- 1 teaspoon vanilla extract
- ¼ teaspoon salt
- ½ cup coarsely chopped pecans
- 2 cups (12 ounces) semisweet chocolate chunks

1. Preheat oven to 350°. In a large bowl, combine cocoa and baking soda; blend ⅓ cup melted butter. Add boiling water; stir until well blended. Stir in sugar, eggs and remaining butter. Add flour, vanilla and salt. Stir in pecans and chocolate chunks.

2. Pour into a greased 13x9-in. baking pan. Bake 35-40 minutes or until brownies begin to pull away from sides of pan. Cool.

CHUNKY BLOND BROWNIES

Every bite of these chewy delights is stuffed with chunks of white and semisweet chocolate and macadamia nuts. It's a potluck offering that really stands out.

—ROSEMARY DREISKE LEMMON, SD

PREP: 15 MIN.
BAKE: 25 MIN. + COOLING
MAKES: 2 DOZEN

- ½ cup butter, softened
- ¾ cup sugar
- ¾ cup packed brown sugar
- 2 eggs
- 2 teaspoons vanilla extract
- 1½ cups all-purpose flour
- 1 teaspoon baking powder
- ½ teaspoon salt
- 1 cup white baking chips
- 1 cup semisweet chocolate chunks
- 1 jar (3 ounces) macadamia nuts or ¾ cup blanched almonds, chopped, divided

1. Preheat oven to 350°. In a large bowl, cream butter and sugars until light and fluffy. Beat in eggs and vanilla. Combine flour, baking powder and salt; gradually add to creamed mixture and mix well. Stir in white chips, chocolate chunks and ½ cup nuts.

2. Spoon into a greased 13x9-in. baking pan; spread over the bottom of pan. Sprinkle with remaining nuts. Bake 25-30 minutes or until top begins to crack and is golden brown. Cool on a wire rack. Cut into bars.

CHOCOLATE MINT BROWNIES

One of the best things about this recipe? The brownies get even better if you leave them in the refrigerator for a day or two.

—HELEN BAINES ELKTON, MD

PREP: 20 MIN. • **BAKE:** 30 MIN. + CHILLING
MAKES: 5-6 DOZEN

- ½ cup butter, softened
- 1 cup sugar
- 4 eggs
- 1 can (16 ounces) chocolate syrup
- 1 teaspoon vanilla extract
- 1 cup all-purpose flour
- ½ teaspoon salt

FILLING

- ½ cup butter, softened
- 2 cups confectioners' sugar
- 1 tablespoon water
- ½ teaspoon mint extract
- 3 drops green food coloring

TOPPING

- 1 package (10 ounces) mint chocolate chips
- ½ cup plus 1 tablespoon butter, cubed

1. Preheat oven to 350°. In a large bowl, cream butter and sugar until light and fluffy. Add eggs, one at a time, beating well after each addition. Beat in syrup and vanilla. Add flour and salt; mix well.

2. Pour into a greased 13x9-in. baking pan. Bake 30 minutes (the top of brownies will still appear wet). Cool on a wire rack.

3. For filling, in a small bowl, cream butter and confectioners' sugar; add water, extract and food coloring until blended. Spread over cooled brownies. Refrigerate until set.

4. For topping, melt chocolate chips and butter. Cool 30 minutes, stirring occasionally. Spread over filling. Chill. Cut into bars. Store in refrigerator.

NOTE *If mint chocolate chips are not available, place 2 cups (12 ounces) semisweet chocolate chips and ¼ teaspoon peppermint extract in a plastic bag; seal and toss to coat. Allow chips to stand for 24-48 hours.*

COOKIE DOUGH BROWNIES

When I take these rich brownies to a get-together, I bring along the recipe, too, because people always ask for it. Folks love the tempting cookie dough filling. Watch these brownies disappear first from the buffet table—even before the entrees!

—WENDY BAILEY ELIDA, OH

PREP: 20 MIN. + CHILLING
BAKE: 30 MIN. + COOLING
MAKES: 3 DOZEN

- 4 **eggs**
- 1 **cup canola oil**
- 2 **cups sugar**
- 2 **teaspoons vanilla extract**
- 1½ **cups all-purpose flour**
- ½ **cup baking cocoa**
- ½ **teaspoon salt**
- ½ **cup chopped walnuts, optional**

FILLING
- ½ **cup butter, softened**
- ½ **cup packed brown sugar**
- ¼ **cup sugar**
- 2 **tablespoons 2% milk**
- 1 **teaspoon vanilla extract**
- 1 **cup all-purpose flour**

GLAZE
- 1 **cup (6 ounces) semisweet chocolate chips**
- 1 **tablespoon shortening**
- ¾ **cup chopped walnuts**

1. Preheat oven to 350°. In a large bowl, beat eggs, oil, sugar and vanilla until well blended. Combine flour, cocoa and salt; gradually beat into egg mixture. Stir in walnuts if desired.

2. Pour into a greased 13x9-in. baking pan. Bake 30 minutes or until brownies test done. Cool completely.

3. For filling, in a large bowl, cream butter and sugars until light and fluffy. Beat in milk and vanilla. Gradually beat in flour. Spread over brownies; chill until firm.

4. For glaze, in a microwave, melt chocolate chips and shortening; stir until smooth. Spread over filling. Immediately sprinkle with nuts, pressing down slightly. Let stand until set.

APPLE CARAMEL CHEESECAKE BARS

Are you a fan of caramel apples, cheesecake and streusel-topped apple pie? This recipe has a bit of them all! I wouldn't blame you for sneaking a bite before the guests arrive.
—**KATHERINE WHITE** CLEMMONS, NC

PREP: 30 MIN. • **BAKE:** 25 MIN. + CHILLING
MAKES: 3 DOZEN

- 2 **cups all-purpose flour**
- ½ **cup packed brown sugar**
- ¾ **cup cold butter, cubed**
- 2 **packages (8 ounces each) cream cheese, softened**
- ½ **cup plus 2 tablespoons sugar, divided**
- 1 **teaspoon vanilla extract**
- 2 **eggs, lightly beaten**
- 3 **medium tart apples, peeled and finely chopped**
- ½ **teaspoon ground cinnamon**
- ¼ **teaspoon ground nutmeg**

STREUSEL
- ¾ **cup all-purpose flour**
- ¾ **cup packed brown sugar**
- ½ **cup quick-cooking oats**
- ⅓ **cup cold butter, cubed**
- ⅓ **cup hot caramel ice cream topping**

1. Preheat oven to 350°. In a small bowl, combine flour and brown sugar; cut in butter until crumbly. Press into a well-greased 13x9-in. baking pan. Bake 15-18 minutes or until lightly browned.
2. Meanwhile, in a large bowl, beat cream cheese, ½ cup sugar and vanilla until smooth. Add eggs; beat on low speed just until combined. Spread over the crust.
3. In a small bowl, toss apples with cinnamon, nutmeg and remaining sugar; spoon over cream cheese layer. In another bowl, mix flour, brown sugar and oats; cut in butter until crumbly. Sprinkle over apple layer.
4. Bake 25-30 minutes or until filling is set. Drizzle with caramel topping; cool in pan on a wire rack 1 hour. Refrigerate at least 2 hours. Cut into bars.

RASPBERRY BARS

While mixing up a batch of basic bars, I was inspired to add raspberry preserves and flaked coconut to the dough and wound up with this family-favorite version.
—**AMANDA DENTON** BARRE, VT

PREP: 20 MIN. • **BAKE:** 30 MIN. + COOLING
MAKES: 3 DOZEN

- ¾ **cup butter, softened**
- 1 **cup sugar**
- 1 **egg**
- ½ **teaspoon vanilla extract**
- 2 **cups all-purpose flour**
- ¼ **teaspoon baking powder**
- 2 **cups flaked coconut, divided**
- ½ **cup chopped walnuts**
- 1 **jar (12 ounces) raspberry preserves**
- 1 **cup white baking chips**

1. Preheat oven to 350°. In a large bowl, cream butter and sugar until light and fluffy. Beat in egg and vanilla. Combine flour and baking powder; gradually add to the creamed mixture and mix well. Stir in 1¼ cups coconut and walnuts.
2. Press three-fourths of the dough into a greased 13x9-in. baking pan. Spread with preserves. Sprinkle with chips and remaining coconut. Crumble remaining dough over the top; press lightly.
3. Bake 30-35 minutes or until golden brown. Cool on a wire rack. Cut into bars.

COOKIE NOTES

_____
_____
_____
_____
_____
_____
_____
_____
_____
_____
_____
_____
_____
_____
_____
_____
_____
_____
_____
_____
_____
_____
_____
_____
_____
_____
_____
_____
_____
_____
_____
_____

BLACKBERRY CHEESECAKE BARS

It's quick and fun to turn cookie dough, berries and two kinds of creamy cheese into these elegant bars.

—TERRI CRANDALL GARDNERVILLE, NV

PREP: 30 MIN. • **BAKE:** 20 MIN. + COOLING
MAKES: 12 SERVINGS

- 1 tube (16½ ounces) refrigerated sugar cookie dough
- 1½ cups ricotta cheese
- 1 carton (8 ounces) mascarpone cheese
- ½ cup sugar
- 2 eggs, lightly beaten
- 3 teaspoons vanilla extract
- 2 teaspoons grated lemon peel
- 1 teaspoon lemon juice
- 1 teaspoon orange juice
- 1 tablespoon amaretto, optional
- 1 cup seedless blackberry spreadable fruit
- 2⅔ cups fresh blackberries

1. Preheat oven to 375°. Let cookie dough stand at room temperature 5 minutes to soften. Press onto bottom and 1 in. up sides of a greased 13x9-in. baking dish. Bake 12-15 minutes or until golden brown. Cool on a wire rack.

2. Meanwhile, in a large bowl, beat ricotta cheese, mascarpone cheese and sugar until blended. Add eggs; beat on low speed just until combined. Stir in vanilla, lemon peel, citrus juices and, if desired, amaretto. Pour into crust.

3. Bake 20-25 minutes or until center is almost set. Cool 1 hour on a wire rack.

4. Place spreadable fruit in a small microwave-safe bowl; microwave on high for 30-45 seconds or until melted. Spread over cheesecake layer; top with blackberries. Refrigerate until serving.

Blackberry
Cheesecake Bars

WARREN'S OATMEAL JAM SQUARES

At 102 years old, I still love to bake. I make these bars in my toaster oven for my fellow residents at our assisted living home.

—WARREN PATRICK TOWNSHEND, VT

PREP: 20 MIN. • **BAKE:** 25 MIN. + COOLING
MAKES: 16 SQUARES

- 1¼ cups quick-cooking oats
- 1¼ cups all-purpose flour
- ½ cup sugar
- ½ teaspoon baking soda
- ¼ teaspoon salt
- ¾ cup butter, melted
- 2 teaspoons vanilla extract
- 1 jar (10 ounces) seedless raspberry jam or jam of your choice
- 4 whole graham crackers, crushed

1. Preheat oven to 350°. In a large bowl, mix the first five ingredients. In a small bowl, mix melted butter and vanilla; add to oats mixture, stirring until crumbly. Reserve 1 cup mixture for topping.

2. Press remaining mixture onto bottom of a greased 9-in.-square baking pan. Spread jam over top to within ½ in. of edges. Add crushed graham crackers to reserved topping; sprinkle over jam.

3. Bake 25-30 minutes or until edges are golden brown. Cool in pan on a wire rack. Cut into squares.

KEY LIME BARS

I love Key lime pie, but sometimes people don't want a whole slice of it. These bars are as creamy and zesty as the pie and also freeze well, so I can keep a stash for times when I need a tart treat.

—KRISTINE STATON BROOMFIELD, CO

PREP: 25 MIN. + COOLING
BAKE: 35 MIN. + CHILLING
MAKES: 3 DOZEN

- 1¼ cups all-purpose flour
- 30 vanilla wafers, broken into pieces
- ½ cup confectioners' sugar
- ½ cup chopped pecans
- ¾ cup cold butter, cubed

CREAM CHEESE LAYER
- 1 package (8 ounces) cream cheese, softened
- ¼ cup sugar
- 2 tablespoons 2% milk
- 1 teaspoon vanilla extract

KEY LIME LAYER
- 1½ cups sugar
- ¼ cup all-purpose flour
- 4 eggs
- ½ cup Key lime juice
  Additional confectioners' sugar

1. Preheat oven to 350°. In a food processor, combine flour, wafers, confectioners' sugar and pecans; cover and process until nuts are fine. Add butter; cover and pulse until crumbly.
2. Press into an ungreased 13x9-in. baking dish. Bake 15-18 minutes or until lightly browned. Cool on a wire rack.
3. In a small bowl, beat cream cheese, sugar, milk and vanilla until blended; spread over crust to edges of pan. In another small bowl, combine sugar and flour; whisk in eggs and lime juice. Gently pour over cream cheese layer.

4. Bake 20-25 minutes longer or until filling is set. Cool on a wire rack. Refrigerate 1 hour or until chilled. Cut into bars. Just before serving, sprinkle with additional confectioners' sugar.

GOLD RUSH BROWNIES

PREP: 5 MIN. • **BAKE:** 25 MIN. + COOLING
MAKES: 1 DOZEN

- 2 cups graham cracker crumbs
- 1 cup (6 ounces) semisweet chocolate chips
- ½ cup chopped pecans
- 1 can (14 ounces) sweetened condensed milk

1. Preheat oven to 350°. In a bowl, combine crumbs, chocolate chips and pecans. Stir in milk until blended (batter will be stiff). Spread into a greased 8-in.-square baking pan.
2. Bake 25-30 minutes or until a toothpick inserted near the center comes out clean. Cool on a wire rack. Cut into bars.

> With six kids to keep an eye on, my mother relied on simple recipes like this. Now my own family can't resist these chewy brownies.
> **—KELLIE ERWIN** WESTERVILLE, OH

CHOCOLATE-PEANUT BUTTER CRUNCH BARS

My twist on Rice Krispies bars includes crunchy crushed pretzels, topped with a creamy peanut butter layer and a rich chocolate one. The result is heavenly.
—SHERRI MELOTIK OAK CREEK, WI

PREP: 20 MIN. + CHILLING • **MAKES:** 3 DOZEN

- 3 **cups miniature pretzels, coarsely chopped**
- 10 **tablespoons butter, divided**
- 1 **package (10½ ounces) miniature marshmallows**
- 3 **cups Rice Krispies**
- ½ **cup light corn syrup, divided**
- ¾ **cup peanut butter chips**
- 1 **cup (6 ounces) semisweet chocolate chips**
- ¼ **cup dry roasted peanuts, chopped**

1. Reserve ⅓ cup chopped pretzels. In a large microwave-safe bowl, microwave 6 tablespoons butter on high for 45-60 seconds or until melted. Stir in marshmallows; cook 1 to 1½ minutes or until marshmallows are melted, stirring every 30 seconds. Stir in Rice Krispies and remaining chopped pretzels. Immediately press into a greased 13x9-in. baking pan.

2. In another microwave-safe bowl, combine 2 tablespoons butter and ¼ cup corn syrup. Microwave, uncovered, on high for 45-60 seconds or until butter is melted, stirring once. Add peanut butter chips; cook 30-40 seconds or until chips are melted, stirring once. Spread over cereal layer.

3. In a microwave-safe bowl, combine remaining corn syrup and remaining butter. Cook on high for 45-60 seconds or until butter is melted, stirring once. Add chocolate chips; cook 30-40 seconds longer or until chips are melted, stirring once. Spread over top.

4. Sprinkle with peanuts and reserved pretzels; press down gently. Cover and refrigerate 30 minutes or until set. Cut into bars. Store in airtight containers.

Chocolate-Peanut Butter
Crunch Bars

PEANUT BUTTER-HAZELNUT BROWNIES

Over the years I'd been adding this and that to my basic brownie recipe—and then I came up with this one!

—DENISE WHEELER NEWAYGO, MI

PREP: 20 MIN. • **BAKE:** 35 MIN. + COOLING
MAKES: 2 DOZEN

- 1 **cup butter, softened**
- 2 **cups sugar**
- 4 **eggs**
- 2 **teaspoons vanilla extract**
- 1 **cup all-purpose flour**
- ¾ **cup baking cocoa**
- ½ **teaspoon baking powder**
  Dash salt
- 1½ **cups coarsely crushed malted milk balls**
- ½ **cup creamy peanut butter**
- ½ **cup Nutella**

1. Preheat oven to 350°. In a large bowl, cream butter and sugar until light and fluffy. Add eggs, one at a time, beating well after each addition. Beat in vanilla. Combine the flour, cocoa, baking powder and salt; gradually add to creamed mixture. Fold in malted milk balls.

2. Spread into a greased 13x9-in. baking pan. In a small microwave-safe bowl, combine peanut butter and Nutella; cover and microwave at 50% power for 1-2 minutes or until smooth, stirring twice. Drizzle over batter; cut through batter with a knife to swirl.

3. Bake 35-40 minutes or until a toothpick inserted near the center comes out clean (do not overbake). Cool on a wire rack.

PUMPKIN CREAM CHEESE BARS

The first time I brought these to a church function, there was barely a crumb left on the platter when it was time to leave.
—**KIM CHAMBERS** LAURELTON, NY

PREP: 25 MIN. • **BAKE:** 35 MIN. + COOLING
MAKES: 2 DOZEN

- 1⅓ cups all-purpose flour
- ¾ cup sugar, divided
- ½ cup packed brown sugar
- ¾ cup cold butter, cubed
- 1 cup old-fashioned oats
- ½ cup chopped pecans
- 1 package (8 ounces) cream cheese, softened, cubed
- 2 teaspoons ground cinnamon
- 1 teaspoon ground allspice
- 1 teaspoon ground cardamom
- 1 can (15 ounces) solid-pack pumpkin
- 1 teaspoon vanilla extract
- 3 eggs, lightly beaten

1. Preheat oven to 350°. In a small bowl, mix flour, ¼ cup sugar and brown sugar; cut in butter until crumbly. Stir in oats and pecans. Reserve 1 cup for topping.
2. Press remaining crumb mixture onto bottom of a greased 13x9-in. baking pan. Bake 15 minutes.
3. In a small bowl, beat cream cheese, spices and remaining sugar until smooth. Beat in pumpkin and vanilla. Add eggs; beat on low speed just until blended. Pour over warm crust; sprinkle with reserved crumb mixture.
4. Bake 20-25 minutes or until a knife inserted near the center comes out clean and filling is set. Cool on a wire rack. Serve or refrigerate, covered, within 2 hours. Cut into bars.

PEANUT BUTTER SQUARES

I grew up in Lancaster County, Pennsylvania, and spent a lot of time in the kitchen with my mom and grandmother making Pennsylvania Dutch classics. This scrumptious recipe is one I adapted to make it my own.
—**RACHEL GREENAWALT KELLER**
ROANOKE, VA

PREP: 20 MIN. + CHILLING
MAKES: 4 DOZEN

- ¾ cup cold butter, cubed
- 2 ounces semisweet chocolate
- 1½ cups graham cracker crumbs (about 24 squares)
- 1 cup flaked coconut
- ½ cup chopped salted peanuts
- ¼ cup toasted wheat germ

FILLING
- 2 packages (8 ounces each) cream cheese, softened
- ¾ cup sugar
- ⅔ cup chunky peanut butter
- 1 teaspoon vanilla extract

TOPPING
- 4 ounces semisweet chocolate, chopped
- ¼ cup butter, cubed

1. In a microwave-safe bowl, melt butter and chocolate; stir until smooth. Stir in the cracker crumbs, coconut, peanuts and wheat germ. Press into a greased 13x9-in. pan. Cover and refrigerate for at least 30 minutes.
2. In a small bowl, combine filling ingredients. Spread over crust. Cover and refrigerate for at least 30 minutes.
3. In a microwave, melt chocolate and butter; stir until smooth. Pour over filling. Cover and refrigerate for at least 30 minutes or until topping is set. Cut into squares. Refrigerate leftovers.

LAYERED GINGERBREAD BARS

PREP: 45 MIN. + CHILLING
BAKE: 20 MIN. + COOLING
MAKES: 3 DOZEN

- ½ cup butter, softened
- ⅔ cup packed brown sugar
- 1 egg
- ⅓ cup molasses
- 1⅔ cups all-purpose flour
- 1⅛ teaspoons ground ginger
- ½ teaspoon each salt, baking soda, ground cinnamon and ground allspice
- ¼ teaspoon ground nutmeg
- ⅛ teaspoon ground cloves

BUTTERCREAM LAYER

- ½ cup sugar
- 3 tablespoons all-purpose flour
- ½ cup 2% milk
- ¾ cup butter, softened
- 1 teaspoon lemon extract

ICING

- ½ cup packed brown sugar
- ⅓ cup heavy whipping cream
- ¼ cup butter, cubed
- 2 tablespoons molasses
- ¼ teaspoon ground allspice
- ¼ teaspoon ground ginger
- ⅛ teaspoon salt
- 2½ cups confectioners' sugar
- 2 tablespoons minced crystallized ginger

1. Preheat oven to 350°. In a large bowl, cream butter and brown sugar. Beat in egg and molasses. Combine flour, ginger, salt, baking soda, cinnamon, allspice, nutmeg and cloves; add to creamed mixture. Pour into a greased 13x9-in. baking dish. Bake 20-25 minutes or until a toothpick comes out clean. Cool on a wire rack.

2. Meanwhile, in a small saucepan, combine sugar and flour. Whisk in milk until smooth. Cook and stir over medium heat until mixture comes to a boil. Reduce heat; cook and stir 2 minutes or until thickened. Remove from heat. Transfer to a small bowl; cover and refrigerate until chilled, about 1 hour.

3. Beat in butter and extract until light and fluffy. Spread over cooled gingerbread. Cover and freeze 15 minutes.

4. For icing, in a small saucepan, combine brown sugar, cream and butter; bring to a boil. Remove from heat; whisk in molasses, allspice, ginger and salt. Transfer to a large bowl; add confectioners' sugar and beat until smooth. Spread over buttercream layer. Sprinkle with crystallized ginger. Refrigerate leftovers.

For a truly special dessert that celebrates the season, bake a batch of these bars. The bottom layer tastes like a cookie, the middle features smooth buttercream and the top layer is a luscious frosting.

—PATTI ANN CHRISTIAN ARARAT, NC

Layered
Gingerbread Bars

CHOCOLATE PECAN PIE BARS

These decadent pecan bars start with a homemade pastry crust and pile on lots of semisweet chocolate. They're perfect for a bake sale or a casual get-together.

—HEATHER BIEDLER MARTINSBURG, WV

PREP: 30 MIN. + CHILLING
BAKE: 50 MIN. + COOLING
MAKES: 3 DOZEN

- 1¾ **cups all-purpose flour**
- ¼ **teaspoon salt**
- ¾ **cup cold butter**
- ¼ **to ½ cup ice water**

FILLING

- 4 **eggs**
- 2 **cups sugar**
- ½ **teaspoon salt**
- 1 **cup all-purpose flour**
- 1 **cup butter, melted and cooled**
- 4 **teaspoons vanilla extract**
- 2⅔ **cups (16 ounces) semisweet chocolate chips**
- 1⅓ **cups chopped pecans**

1. In a small bowl, mix flour and salt; cut in butter until crumbly. Gradually add ice water, tossing with a fork until dough holds together when pressed. Shape into a disk; wrap in plastic wrap. Refrigerate 1 hour or overnight.

2. Preheat oven to 350°. On a lightly floured surface, roll dough to fit bottom of a 13x9-in. baking pan; press into pan. Refrigerate while preparing filling.

3. In a large bowl, beat eggs, sugar and salt on high speed 2 minutes. Stir in flour, melted butter and vanilla. Fold in chocolate chips. Pour over pastry; sprinkle with pecans.

4. Cover loosely with foil. Place on a lower oven rack; bake 20 minutes. Bake, uncovered, 30 minutes longer or until top is golden brown and a knife inserted near the center comes out clean.

5. Cool in pan on a wire rack. Cut into bars. Refrigerate leftovers.

MACADAMIA LEMON BARS

These bars get enthusiastic thumbs up from my friends and family. I make them for almost all of our gatherings.
—**EDIE DESPAIN** LOGAN, UT

PREP: 25 MIN. • **BAKE:** 10 MIN. + COOLING
MAKES: 1 DOZEN

- 1 **cup all-purpose flour**
- ¼ **cup confectioners' sugar**
- ½ **cup butter, melted**
- ¼ **cup chopped macadamia nuts**

FILLING

- 1 **cup sugar**
- 2 **tablespoons all-purpose flour**
- ½ **teaspoon baking powder**
- ¼ **teaspoon salt**
- 2 **eggs**
- 2 **tablespoons lemon juice**
- 2 **teaspoons grated lemon peel**
- 2 **tablespoons chopped macadamia nuts**
  Confectioners' sugar

1. Preheat oven to 350°. In a large bowl, mix flour, confectioners' sugar and melted butter until crumbly; stir in nuts. Press onto bottom and ½ in. up sides of a greased 8-in.-square baking dish. Bake 15-20 minutes or until light brown.
2. Meanwhile, in a small bowl, whisk sugar, flour, baking powder and salt.

Beat in eggs, lemon juice and lemon peel until blended.
3. Pour over hot crust. Sprinkle with nuts. Bake 10-15 minutes or until lightly browned. Cool completely on a wire rack. Cut into bars. Sprinkle with confectioners' sugar. Refrigerate leftovers.

MACADAMIA NUT ORIGINS

The macadamia nut tree originated in Queensland, Australia, and was brought to Hawaii in 1882. Today, almost all of the world's macadamias are grown on the Big Island.

COOKIE NOTES

ALMOND APRICOT BARS

Apricot jam puts the fruit punch in these sweet and slightly tangy bars, but feel free to use seedless raspberry jam if you prefer.

—OLGA WOLKOSKY RICHMOND, BC

PREP: 15 MIN.
BAKE: 45 MIN. + COOLING
MAKES: 1½ DOZEN

- **2 cups white baking chips, divided**
- **½ cup butter, softened**
- **½ cup sugar**
- **2 eggs**
- **1 teaspoon vanilla extract**
- **1 cup all-purpose flour**
- **¾ cup apricot jam**
- **½ cup sliced almonds**

1. Preheat the oven to 325°. In a microwave, melt 1 cup chips; stir until smooth. Set aside.

2. In a large bowl, cream butter and sugar until light and fluffy. Add eggs, one at a time, beating well after each addition. Beat in melted chips and vanilla. Gradually beat in flour. Spread half of the batter into a greased 8-in-square baking dish. Bake 15-20 minutes or until golden brown. Spread with jam.

3. Stir remaining chips into remaining batter. Drop by tablespoonfuls over jam; carefully spread over top. Sprinkle with almonds. Bake 30-35 minutes or until golden brown. Cool completely on a wire rack. Cut into squares; cut squares in half.

PUMPKIN BARS WITH BROWNED BUTTER FROSTING

I based this recipe on one my grandmother used to make. When preparing the frosting, make sure you remove the butter from the heat as soon as it starts to brown. Do not use margarine as a substitute for butter in the frosting.

—MARY WILHELM SPARTA, WI

PREP: 30 MIN. • **BAKE:** 20 MIN. + COOLING
MAKES: 2 DOZEN

1½ cups sugar
1 cup canned pumpkin
½ cup orange juice
½ cup canola oil
2 eggs
2 teaspoons grated orange peel
2 cups all-purpose flour
2 teaspoons baking powder
2 teaspoons pumpkin pie spice
1 teaspoon baking soda
¼ teaspoon salt

FROSTING
⅔ cup butter, cubed
4 cups confectioners' sugar
1 teaspoon vanilla extract
4 to 6 tablespoons 2% milk

1. Preheat oven to 350°. Grease a 15x10x1-in. baking pan. In a large bowl, beat the first six ingredients until well blended. In another bowl, whisk flour, baking powder, pie spice, baking soda and salt; gradually beat into pumpkin mixture.

2. Transfer to prepared pan. Bake 18-22 minutes or until a toothpick inserted in center comes out clean. Cool completely in pan on a wire rack.

3. In a small heavy saucepan, melt butter over medium heat. Heat 5-7 minutes or until golden brown, stirring constantly. Transfer to a large bowl. Gradually beat in confectioners' sugar, vanilla and enough milk to reach desired consistency. Spread over bars; let stand until set.

YUMMY COOKIE BARS

A co-worker at school gave me this recipe, and it's always a big hit. I find the bars are easier to cut if you make them a day in advance and let them sit overnight.
—**TERESA HAMMAN** SLAYTON, MN

PREP: 20 MIN. • **BAKE:** 25 MIN. + COOLING
MAKES: 2 DOZEN

- 1 **package white cake mix (regular size)**
- ½ **cup canola oil**
- 2 **eggs**
- ½ **cup butter, cubed**
- ½ **cup milk chocolate chips**
- ½ **cup peanut butter chips**
- 1 **can (14 ounces) sweetened condensed milk**

1. Preheat oven to 350°. In a large bowl, combine cake mix, oil and eggs. Press half of dough into a greased 13x9-in. baking pan.

2. In a small microwave-safe bowl, melt butter and chips; stir until smooth. Stir in milk. Pour over crust. Drop remaining dough by teaspoonfuls over the top.

3. Bake 25-30 minutes or until edges are golden brown. Cool completely on a wire rack before cutting into bars.

RASPBERRY TRUFFLE BROWNIES

Each rich, fudgy brownie is bursting with fresh, plump red raspberries and topped with a dreamy ganache. This recipe is a little piece of heaven on a plate for chocolate lovers of all ages!

—**AGNES WARD** STRATFORD, ON

PREP: 30 MIN.
BAKE: 25 MIN. + CHILLING
MAKES: 1 DOZEN

- **6 ounces bittersweet chocolate, chopped**
- **½ cup butter, cubed**
- **2 eggs**
- **1 cup sugar**
- **1 teaspoon vanilla extract**
- **1 cup all-purpose flour**
- **¼ teaspoon baking soda**
- **¼ teaspoon salt**
- **1 cup fresh raspberries**

FROSTING
- **6 ounces bittersweet chocolate, chopped**
- **¾ cup heavy whipping cream**
- **2 tablespoons seedless raspberry jam**
- **1 teaspoon vanilla extract**
- **12 fresh raspberries**

1. Preheat oven to 350°. In a microwave, melt chocolate and butter; stir until smooth. In a large bowl, beat eggs, sugar and vanilla. Stir in chocolate mixture. Combine flour, baking soda and salt; gradually add to chocolate mixture just until combined. Gently fold in raspberries.

2. Spread into a greased 9-in.-square baking pan. Bake 25-30 minutes or until a toothpick inserted near the center comes out clean (do not overbake). Cool on a wire rack.

3. For frosting, in a microwave-safe bowl, combine chocolate, cream and jam. Microwave at 50% power 2-3 minutes or until smooth, stirring twice. Transfer to a small bowl; stir in vanilla. Place in a bowl of ice water; stir 3-5 minutes. With a hand mixer, beat on medium speed until soft peaks form.

4. Cut a small hole in a corner of a heavy-duty resealable plastic bag; insert #825 star tip. Fill with ½ cup frosting. Spread remaining frosting over brownies. Cut into 12 bars. Pipe a chocolate rosette in the center of each brownie; top with a raspberry. Cover and refrigerate 30 minutes or until frosting is set. Refrigerate leftovers.

BEATING FOR SOFT PEAKS

When a recipe calls for soft peaks, you should whip until you can lift the beater from the mixture and the points of the peaks curl over.

CHERRY BARS

Whip up a pan of these cheery treats in just 20 minutes with pantry staples. Don't be surprised if they become one of your family's favorite desserts.

—**JANE KAMP** GRAND RAPIDS, MI

PREP: 20 MIN. • **BAKE:** 30 MIN. + COOLING
MAKES: 5 DOZEN

- 1 **cup butter, softened**
- 2 **cups sugar**
- 1 **teaspoon salt**
- 4 **eggs**
- 1 **teaspoon vanilla extract**
- ¼ **teaspoon almond extract**
- 3 **cups all-purpose flour**
- 2 **cans (21 ounces each) cherry pie filling**

GLAZE

- 1 **cup confectioners' sugar**
- ½ **teaspoon vanilla extract**
- ½ **teaspoon almond extract**
- 2 **to 3 tablespoons milk**

1. Preheat oven to 350°. In a large bowl, cream butter, sugar and salt until light and fluffy. Add eggs, one at a time, beating well after each addition. Beat in extracts. Gradually add flour.
2. Spread 3 cups dough into a greased 15x10x1-in. baking pan. Spread with pie filling. Drop remaining dough by teaspoonfuls over filling. Bake 30-35 minutes or until golden brown. Cool completely in pan on a wire rack.
3. In a small bowl, mix confectioners' sugar, extracts and enough milk to reach desired consistency; drizzle over top.

WHITE BROWNIES

I use white chocolate and white baking chips to give traditional brownies a delicious twist. These chewy snacks will satisfy even an ardent chocolate enthusiast.

—**GENEVA MAYER** OLNEY, IL

PREP: 20 MIN. + COOLING • **BAKE:** 40 MIN.
MAKES: ABOUT 4 DOZEN

- 6 **ounces white baking chocolate, chopped**
- 1 **cup butter, cubed**
- 6 **eggs**
- 3 **cups sugar**
- 2 **teaspoons vanilla extract**
- 3 **cups all-purpose flour**
- 1 **teaspoon baking powder**
- ½ **teaspoon salt**
- 1 **package (10 to 12 ounces) white baking chips**
- 1 **cup chopped pecans**

1. In a double boiler or microwave, melt chocolate and butter; cool for 20 minutes.
2. Preheat oven to 350°. In a large bowl, beat eggs and sugar until thick and lemon-colored, about 4 minutes. Gradually beat in melted chocolate and vanilla. Combine flour, baking powder and salt; gradually add to chocolate mixture. Stir in chips and pecans.
3. Pour into a greased 15x10x1-in. baking pan. Bake 40-45 minutes or until golden brown. Cool on a wire rack.

CHERRY WALNUT SQUARES

I call these my naughty-but-nice bars. Packed with dried cherries, white chocolate chips and chopped walnuts, they're very indulgent and oh so good!

—LISA SPEER PALM BEACH, FL

PREP: 25 MIN. BAKE: 25 MIN. + COOLING
MAKES: 6½ DOZEN

- ¾ cup butter, softened
- ⅓ cup packed brown sugar
- 2 tablespoons plus 1½ teaspoons sugar
- ⅛ teaspoon almond extract
- 2 cups all-purpose flour
- ⅛ teaspoon salt

FILLING

- 1 cup plus 2 tablespoons packed brown sugar
- ¾ cup butter, cubed
- ¼ cup light corn syrup
- 2 tablespoons heavy whipping cream
- ¼ teaspoon salt
- 2¾ cups chopped walnuts, divided
- 1 cup dried cherries, chopped
- 2½ teaspoons vanilla extract
- ¾ cup white baking chips

1. Preheat oven to 375°. In a large bowl, cream the butter, sugars and extract until light and fluffy. Combine the flour and salt; gradually add to creamed mixture and mix well. Press onto the bottom of an ungreased 13x9-in. baking pan. Bake 8-10 minutes or until edges begin to brown.

2. Meanwhile, in a large saucepan, combine the brown sugar, butter, corn syrup, cream and salt. Bring to boil over medium heat, stirring constantly. Reduce heat; cook and stir 4 minutes or until slightly thickened.

3. Remove from the heat. Stir in 2½ cups walnuts, cherries and vanilla; spread over crust. Bake 15-20 minutes or until bubbly. Sprinkle with baking chips and remaining walnuts; lightly press into filling. Cool on a wire rack. Cut into bars.

_____
_____
_____
_____
_____
_____
_____
_____
_____
_____
_____
_____
_____
_____
_____
_____
_____
_____
_____
_____
_____
_____
_____
_____
_____
_____
_____
_____
_____
_____
_____

BLUEBERRY CRUMB BARS

PREP: 20 MIN. • **BAKE:** 20 MIN. + COOLING
MAKES: 1 DOZEN

- 1 **package yellow cake mix (regular size)**
- 2½ **cups old-fashioned oats**
- ¾ **cup butter, melted**
- 1 **jar (12 ounces) blueberry preserves**
- ⅓ **cup fresh blueberries**
- 1 **tablespoon lemon juice**
- ⅓ **cup finely chopped pecans**
- 1 **teaspoon ground cinnamon**

1. Preheat oven to 350°. In a large bowl, combine cake mix, oats and butter until crumbly. Press 3 cups into a greased 9-in.-square baking pan. Bake 15 minutes. Cool on a wire rack 5 minutes.

2. Meanwhile, in a small bowl, combine preserves, blueberries and lemon juice. Spread over crust. Stir pecans and cinnamon into remaining crumb mixture. Sprinkle over top.

3. Bake 18-20 minutes or until lightly browned. Cool on a wire rack before cutting into bars.

Think of these bars as a blueberry crisp turned into a hand-held treat. Oats and fresh berries come together for a sweet, no-fuss dessert that's perfect for summer.
—**BLAIR LONERGAN** ROCHELLE, VA

Blueberry
Crumb Bars

CINNAMON NUT BARS

Classic bar meets good-for-you ingredients in this new spin on a traditional recipe. If you can resist temptation, store the bars in a tin for a day (after they've cooled) to allow the flavors to meld. I think they taste even better the next day.

—HEIDI LINDSEY PRAIRIE DU SAC, WI

PREP: 20 MIN.
BAKE: 15 MIN. + COOLING
MAKES: 2 DOZEN

- ½ **cup whole wheat flour**
- ½ **cup all-purpose flour**
- ½ **cup sugar**
- 1½ **teaspoons ground cinnamon**
- 1¼ **teaspoons baking powder**
- ¼ **teaspoon baking soda**
- 1 **egg, beaten**
- ⅓ **cup canola oil**
- ¼ **cup unsweetened applesauce**
- ¼ **cup honey**
- 1 **cup chopped walnuts**

ICING

- 1 **cup confectioners' sugar**
- 2 **tablespoons butter, melted**
- 1 **teaspoon vanilla extract**
- 1 **tablespoon water**
- 2 **tablespoons honey**

1. Preheat oven to 350°. In a large bowl, combine flours, sugar, cinnamon, baking powder and baking soda. In another bowl, combine egg, oil, applesauce and honey. Stir into dry ingredients just until moistened. Fold in walnuts.

2. Spread batter into a 13x9-in. baking pan coated with cooking spray. Bake 15-20 minutes or until a toothpick inserted near center comes out clean.

3. Combine icing ingredients; spread over warm bars. Cool completely before cutting into bars.

CARAMEL TOFFEE BROWNIES

I love to make up recipes for things I'm craving, like chocolate, toffee and caramel. All three of them came together in this brownie for one sensational treat, which I frequently bake to add to care packages for family and friends.

—BRENDA CAUGHELL DURHAM, NC

PREP: 30 MIN. • **BAKE:** 40 MIN. + COOLING
MAKES: 2 DOZEN

CARAMEL LAYER
- ½ cup butter, softened
- ⅓ cup sugar
- ⅓ cup packed brown sugar
- 1 egg
- ½ teaspoon vanilla extract
- 1 cup all-purpose flour
- ½ teaspoon baking soda
- ¼ teaspoon salt
- ½ cup caramel ice cream topping
- 2 tablespoons 2% milk
- 1 cup toffee bits

BROWNIE LAYER
- 1 cup butter, cubed
- 4 ounces unsweetened chocolate
- 4 eggs, lightly beaten
- 2 cups sugar
- 2 teaspoons vanilla extract
- 2 cups all-purpose flour

1. Preheat oven to 350°. In a large bowl, cream butter and sugars until light and fluffy; beat in egg and vanilla. Combine flour, baking soda and salt; gradually add to creamed mixture and mix well. In a small bowl, combine caramel topping and milk; add to the batter and mix well. Fold in toffee bits; set aside.

2. In a microwave, melt butter and chocolate. Beat in eggs, sugar and vanilla; gradually beat in flour.

3. Spread half of brownie batter into a greased 13x9-in. baking pan. Drop caramel batter by spoonfuls onto brownie batter; swirl to combine. Drop remaining brownie batter on top.

4. Bake 40-45 minutes or until a toothpick inserted in center comes out clean. Cool on a wire rack.

COOKIE NOTES

CAPPUCCINO BROWNIES

There's something magical in coffee that intensifies the flavor of chocolate. These three-layer wonders freeze well, but somehow most of them seem to disappear before they reach the freezer!

—SUSIE JONES BUHL, ID

PREP: 30 MIN. + CHILLING
BAKE: 25 MIN. + COOLING
MAKES: 2 DOZEN

- 8 **ounces bittersweet chocolate, chopped**
- ¾ **cup butter, cut up**
- 2 **tablespoons instant coffee granules**
- 1 **tablespoon hot water**
- 4 **eggs**
- 1½ **cups sugar**
- 2 **teaspoons vanilla extract**
- 1 **cup all-purpose flour**
- ½ **teaspoon salt**
- 1 **cup chopped walnuts**

TOPPING
- 1 **package (8 ounces) cream cheese, softened**
- 6 **tablespoons butter, softened**
- 1½ **cups confectioners' sugar**
- 1 **teaspoon ground cinnamon**
- 1 **teaspoon vanilla extract**

GLAZE
- 4 **teaspoons instant coffee granules**
- 1 **tablespoon hot water**
- 5 **ounces bittersweet chocolate, chopped**
- 2 **tablespoons butter**
- ½ **cup heavy whipping cream**

1. Preheat the oven to 350°. In a microwave, melt chocolate and butter; stir until smooth. Cool slightly. Dissolve coffee granules in hot water. In a large bowl, beat eggs and sugar. Stir in vanilla, chocolate mixture and coffee mixture. Combine flour and salt; gradually add to chocolate mixture until blended. Fold in walnuts.

2. Transfer to a greased and floured 13x9-in. baking pan. Bake 25-30 minutes or until a toothpick inserted near the center comes out clean. Cool completely on a wire rack.

3. For topping, in a large bowl, beat cream cheese and butter until blended. Add confectioners' sugar, cinnamon and vanilla; beat on low speed until combined. Spread over bars. Refrigerate until firm, about 1 hour.

4. For glaze, dissolve coffee granules in hot water. In a microwave, melt chocolate and butter; cool slightly. Stir in cream and coffee mixture. Spread over cream cheese layer. Let stand until set. Cut into bars. Refrigerate leftovers.

FREEZE OPTION *Cover and freeze for up to 1 month. To use, thaw at room temperature. Cut into bars. Refrigerate leftovers.*

TOFFEE CHEESECAKE BARS

These melt-in-your-mouth snacks are absolutely divine—almost everyone wants seconds. I bet the recipe will become a real keeper for your collection.

—**EDIE DESPAIN** LOGAN, UT

PREP: 25 MIN. • **BAKE:** 20 MIN. + CHILLING
MAKES: 2½ DOZEN

- 1 cup all-purpose flour
- ¾ cup confectioners' sugar
- ⅓ cup baking cocoa
- ⅛ teaspoon baking soda
- ½ cup cold butter
- 1 package (8 ounces) reduced-fat cream cheese
- 1 can (14 ounces) sweetened condensed milk
- 2 eggs, lightly beaten
- 1 teaspoon vanilla extract
- 1¼ cups milk chocolate English toffee bits, divided

1. Preheat oven to 350°. In a small bowl, combine flour, confectioners' sugar, cocoa and baking soda. Cut in butter until mixture resembles coarse crumbs. Press onto the bottom of an ungreased 13x9-in. baking dish. Bake 12-15 minutes or until set.

2. In a large bowl, beat cream cheese until fluffy. Add milk, eggs and vanilla; beat until smooth. Stir in ¾ cup toffee bits. Pour over crust. Bake 18-22 minutes longer or until center is almost set.

3. Cool on a wire rack 15 minutes. Sprinkle with remaining toffee bits; cool completely. Cover and refrigerate 8 hours or overnight.

Triple Chocolate
Cookie Mix

Homemade
Mixes

TRIPLE CHOCOLATE COOKIE MIX

Everyone likes a good old-fashioned cookie mix—and this one is especially popular with chocoholics.

—PATRICIA SWART GALLOWAY, NJ

PREP: 30 MIN. • **BAKE:** 15 MIN./BATCH
MAKES: 5 DOZEN

- 2¼ **cups all-purpose flour, divided**
- 1 **teaspoon baking powder**
- ½ **teaspoon salt**
- ½ **teaspoon baking soda**
- ½ **cup baking cocoa**
- 1 **cup packed brown sugar**
- ½ **cup sugar**
- ¾ **cup semisweet chocolate chips**
- ¾ **cup white baking chips**

ADDITIONAL INGREDIENTS
- ¾ **cup butter, melted and cooled**
- 3 **eggs**
- 3 **teaspoons vanilla extract**

1. In a small bowl, whisk 1¼ cups flour, baking powder, salt and baking soda. In another bowl, whisk cocoa and remaining flour. In an airtight container, layer half of flour mixture and half of cocoa mixture; repeat. Layer sugars and chips in the order listed. Cover and store in a cool, dry place up to 3 months. Makes: 1 batch (about 5 cups).

2. To prepare cookies: Preheat oven to 350°. In a large bowl, beat butter, eggs and vanilla until well blended. Add cookie mix; mix well.

3. Drop by tablespoonfuls 2 in. apart on ungreased baking sheets. Bake 12-14 minutes or until firm. Remove from pans to wire racks to cool. Store in an airtight container.

COWBOY COOKIE MIX

Since half the fun of cookies is baking them, I give this lovely mix often. The ingredients look so pretty in a jar—and the aroma drifting from the oven while the cookies bake is just terrific!

—ROSEMARY GRIFFITH TULSA, OK

PREP: 20 MIN. + CHILLING
BAKE: 15 MIN./BATCH
MAKES: ABOUT 3½ DOZEN

- 1⅓ **cups quick-cooking oats**
- 1⅓ **cups all-purpose flour**
- 1 **teaspoon baking powder**
- 1 **teaspoon baking soda**
- ¼ **teaspoon salt**
- ½ **cup chopped pecans**
- 1 **cup (6 ounces) semisweet chocolate chips**
- ½ **cup packed brown sugar**
- ½ **cup sugar**

ADDITIONAL INGREDIENTS
- ½ **cup butter, melted**
- 1 **egg, lightly beaten**
- 1 **teaspoon vanilla extract**

1. Pour oats into a wide-mouth 1-qt. glass container with a tight-fitting lid. Combine flour, baking powder, baking soda and salt; place on top of oats. Layer with pecans, chocolate chips, brown sugar and sugar, packing each layer tightly (do not mix). Cover and store in a cool, dry place for up to 6 months. Makes: 1 batch.

2. To prepare cookies: Pour cookie mix into a large bowl; stir to combine ingredients. Beat in butter, egg and vanilla. Cover and refrigerate for 30 minutes.

3. Preheat oven to 350°. Roll into 1-in. balls. Place 2 in. apart on greased baking sheets. Bake 11-13 minutes or until set. Remove to wire racks to cool.

SAND ART BROWNIE MIX

These brownies are so good that I always keep a few jars on hand to add to gift baskets or use as hostess gifts. It's easy to decorate the jars by covering the lids with holiday material and tying a ribbon around the top to hold it in place.

—CLAUDIA TEMPLE SUTTON, WV

PREP: 15 MIN.
BAKE: 25 MIN. + COOLING
MAKES: 16 SERVINGS

- 1 cup plus 2 tablespoons all-purpose flour
- ½ teaspoon salt
- ⅔ cup packed brown sugar
- ⅔ cup sugar
- ⅓ cup baking cocoa
- ½ cup semisweet chocolate chips
- ½ cup white baking chips
- ½ cup chopped pecans

ADDITIONAL INGREDIENTS

- 3 eggs
- ⅔ cup canola oil
- 1 teaspoon vanilla extract

1. In a small bowl, combine flour and salt. In a 1-qt. glass container, layer flour mixture, brown sugar, sugar, cocoa, chips and pecans. Cover and store in a cool, dry place up to 6 months. Makes: 1 batch (about 4 cups total).

2. To prepare brownies: Preheat oven to 350°. In a large bowl, whisk eggs, oil and vanilla. Add brownie mix; stir until blended.

3. Spread into a greased 9-in.-square baking pan. Bake 25-30 minutes or until a toothpick inserted near the center comes out clean (do not overbake). Cool on a wire rack.

MIX FOR CRANBERRY LEMONADE BARS

PREP: 20 MIN. • **BAKE:** 20 MIN. + COOLING
MAKES: 2 DOZEN

- 2¼ cups all-purpose flour
- 1 cup sugar
- ¾ teaspoon baking soda
- ½ teaspoon salt
- 1 cup dried cranberries

ADDITIONAL INGREDIENTS

- 1 egg
- ½ cup butter, softened
- ⅓ cup frozen lemonade concentrate, thawed
- 1 tablespoon grated lemon peel
  Confectioners' sugar

1. In a 1-qt. glass jar, layer the first five ingredients in order listed, packing well between each layer. Cover tightly. Store in a cool, dry place up to 6 months.

2. To prepare bars: Preheat oven to 350°. In a large bowl, combine egg, butter, lemonade concentrate, lemon peel and lemon bar mix. Press into a greased 13x9-in. baking pan. Bake 20-25 minutes or until lightly browned. Cool on a wire rack. Dust with confectioners' sugar; cut into bars.

> I recently put all of our family's special recipes in a cookbook to pass down. These tangy bars were part of the collection.
>
> **—SUZETTE JURY** KEENE, CA

CHOCOLATE CHIP COOKIE MIX

When it comes to baking for a crowd, these cookies are perfect, because you can prepare the mix ahead and store it for months. Also, you can bake a couple batches of cookies at a time and freeze.

—HELEN WORONIK SALEM, CT

PREP: 15 MIN. • **BAKE:** 10 MIN./BATCH
MAKES: 5 DOZEN PER BATCH

COOKIE MIX

- 9 **cups all-purpose flour**
- 4 **teaspoons baking soda**
- 2 **teaspoons salt**
- 3 **cups packed brown sugar**
- 3 **cups sugar**
- 4 **cups shortening**

COOKIES

- 6 **cups Cookie Mix (to the left)**
- 1 **teaspoon vanilla extract**
- 2 **eggs, beaten**
- 2 **cups (12 ounces) semisweet chocolate chips**

1. Thoroughly combine dry ingredients; cut in shortening until crumbly. Store in an airtight container in a cool, dry place up to 6 months. Makes: 3 batches (18 cups mix).

2. To make cookies: Preheat oven to 375°. In a bowl, combine mix, vanilla and eggs. Fold in chocolate chips. Drop by tablespoonfuls ½ in. apart onto greased baking sheets. Bake 10-12 minutes or until golden brown. Remove to wire racks to cool.

Crisp Sugar
Cookie Mix

CRISP SUGAR COOKIE MIX

I've relied on this mix for these light sugar cookies for years, even selling it at bazaars. I package it in a plastic bag tied with a pretty ribbon and attach a cookie cutter and copy of the recipe.

—ENEATHA ATTIG SECREST MATTOON, IL

PREP: 20 MIN. • **BAKE:** 10 MIN./BATCH
MAKES: ABOUT 4 DOZEN PER BATCH

- 5 **cups all-purpose flour**
- 3 **cups confectioners' sugar**
- 2 **teaspoons baking soda**
- 2 **teaspoons cream of tartar**

ADDITIONAL INGREDIENTS (FOR EACH BATCH)

- 1 **cup butter, softened**
- 1 **egg**
- 1 **teaspoon vanilla extract**
- ½ **teaspoon almond extract**
  Colored sugar, optional

1. In a large bowl, combine the first four ingredients; mix well. Store in an airtight container in a cool, dry place up to 6 months. Makes: 2 batches (8 cups total).

2. To prepare cookies: In a large bowl, cream butter. Beat in egg and extracts. Gradually add 4 cups cookie mix; mix well. Cover and chill 2-3 hours or overnight.

3. Preheat oven to 375°. On a lightly floured surface, roll out dough to ⅛-in. thickness. Cut with a 2½-in. cookie cutter dipped in flour. Place 1 in. apart on ungreased baking sheets. Sprinkle with colored sugar if desired. Bake 7-9 minutes or until the edges are lightly browned. Cool on wire racks.

NOTE *Omit colored sugar if you want to frost the cookies.*

COOKIE NOTES

For variety, I add extra goodies to the simple brownie mix to make this gift. It's a quick answer to dessert when life is busy or unexpected company drops by.
—**KATHRYN ROACH** EDGEMONT, AR

BASIC BROWNIE MIX

START TO FINISH: 5 MIN.
MAKES: 9 SERVINGS

- 5 **cups sugar**
- 3 **cups all-purpose flour**
- 1 **can (8 ounces) baking cocoa**
- 1 **teaspoon salt**

ADDITIONAL INGREDIENTS (FOR EACH BATCH OF BROWNIES)

- ½ **cup butter, melted**
- 2 **eggs, lightly beaten**
- 1 **tablespoon water**
- ½ **teaspoon vanilla extract**

FOR CARAMEL-NUT BROWNIES

- ¼ **cup caramel ice cream topping**
- ¾ **cup chopped pecans, toasted, divided**

FOR CHERRY OR CRANBERRY BROWNIES

- ½ **cup dried cherries or cranberries**
- ½ **cup water**
  Frosting of your choice, optional

1. In a large bowl, combine sugar, flour, cocoa and salt. Store in an airtight container in a cool, dry place for up to 6 months. Makes: 5 batches (about 10 cups total).

2. To prepare basic brownies: Preheat oven to 350°. In a large bowl, combine 2 cups brownie mix, butter, eggs, water and vanilla. Pour into a greased 8-in.-square baking dish. Bake 25-30 minutes or until a toothpick inserted near the center comes out clean. Cool on a wire rack.

3. To prepare caramel-nut brownies: Prepare basic brownie batter. Pour half into a greased 8-in.-square baking dish. Drizzle with caramel topping and sprinkle with ½ cup pecans. Top with remaining batter and pecans. Bake and cool as directed.

4. To prepare cherry brownies: In a small saucepan, bring the cherries and water to a boil. Remove from heat; let stand 5 minutes. Drain and pat dry. Prepare basic brownie batter; stir in cherries. Pour mixture into a greased 8-in.-square baking dish. Bake and cool as directed. Frost if desired.

PEPPERMINT-FUDGE BROWNIE MIX

This mix is just beautiful when packaged as a gift, with the crushed peppermints sparkling against the dark chocolate. I put the jar in a gift basket with red and white napkins and the baking instructions printed on an index card.

—BARBARA BURGE LOS GATOS, CA

PREP: 25 MIN. • **BAKE:** 25 MIN. + COOLING
MAKES: 2 DOZEN

- 1 **cup all-purpose flour**
- 1 **cup baking cocoa**
- 1¾ **cups sugar**
- 1 **cup (6 ounces) semisweet chocolate chips**
- ½ **cup crushed peppermint candies**

ADDITIONAL INGREDIENTS

- 1 **cup butter, softened**
- 4 **eggs**
- ½ **cup chopped walnuts, optional**

1. In a 1-qt. glass jar, layer flour, cocoa, sugar, chocolate chips and peppermint candies, pressing down to fit if needed. Cover and store in a cool, dry place for up to 6 months. Makes: 1 batch (about 4 cups mix).

2. To prepare brownies: Preheat oven to 325°. In a large bowl, beat the butter until creamy. Add eggs, one at a time, until blended. Gradually add brownie mix, mixing well. If desired, stir in walnuts. Spread into a greased 13x9-in. baking pan.

3. Bake 25-30 minutes or until a toothpick inserted in center comes out clean (do not overbake). Cool completely in pan on a wire rack.

CRANBERRY-CHOCOLATE CHIP COOKIE MIX

I give this cookie mix for teacher gifts and Christmas stocking stuffers. One teacher told me they were the best cookies she'd ever made!

—SHELLEY FRIESEN LEDUC, AB

PREP: 15 MIN. • **BAKE:** 10 MIN./BATCH
MAKES: 2½ DOZEN

- 1¼ cups all-purpose flour
- 1 teaspoon baking soda
- ½ teaspoon salt
- ½ teaspoon ground cinnamon
- ¾ cup packed brown sugar
- 1 cup (6 ounces) semisweet chocolate chips
- ½ cup dried cranberries
- ½ cup chopped walnuts
- ½ cup quick-cooking oats

ADDITIONAL INGREDIENTS

- ⅔ cup butter, softened
- 1 egg
- ¾ teaspoon vanilla extract

1. In a small bowl, combine flour, baking soda, salt and cinnamon. In a 1-qt. glass container, layer the flour mixture, brown sugar, ½ cup chocolate chips, cranberries, walnuts, oats and remaining chips. Cover and store in a cool, dry place up to 6 months. Makes: 1 batch (about 4 cups total).

2. To prepare cookies: Preheat oven to 350°. In a large bowl, beat butter, egg and vanilla until blended. Add cookie mix and mix well.

3. Drop by rounded tablespoonfuls 2 in. apart onto ungreased baking sheets. Bake 10-15 minutes or until golden brown. Remove to wire racks.

MOLASSES COOKIE MIX

Just watch: These classic treats will become a big hit with your family and friends!

—BARBARA STEWART PORTLAND, CT

START TO FINISH: 10 MIN.
MAKES: ABOUT 4 DOZEN PER BATCH

- 6 **cups all-purpose flour**
- 3 **cups sugar**
- 1 **tablespoon baking soda**
- 1 **tablespoon baking powder**
- 1 **tablespoon ground ginger**
- 1 **tablespoon ground cinnamon**
- 1½ **teaspoons ground nutmeg**
- ¾ **teaspoon ground cloves**
- ½ **teaspoon ground allspice**

ADDITIONAL INGREDIENTS (FOR EACH BATCH)

- ¾ **cup butter, softened**
- 1 **egg**
- ¼ **cup molasses**
  Additional sugar

1. In a large bowl, combine the first nine ingredients. Divide into three batches; store in airtight containers in a cool, dry place up to 6 months. Makes: 3 batches (9 cups total).

2. To prepare cookies: Preheat oven to 375°. In a large bowl, cream butter until light and fluffy. Add egg and molasses; mix well. Add 3 cups cookie mix; beat until smooth.

3. Shape into 1-in. balls and roll in sugar. Place 2 in. apart on ungreased baking sheets. Bake 9-11 minutes or until the edges are firm and the surface cracks. Cool on wire racks.

SPICY OATMEAL COOKIE MIX

Brown sugar and spice and everything nice—including cinnamon, coconut, oats, chocolate and caramel—are layered together in jars for ready-to-bake cookies. Give these out any time of the year.

—TASTE OF HOME TEST KITCHEN

PREP: 15 MIN. • **BAKE:** 10 MIN./BATCH
MAKES: ABOUT 3½ DOZEN

- 1 **cup all-purpose flour**
- 1 **teaspoon ground cinnamon**
- ¾ **teaspoon baking soda**
- ¼ **teaspoon salt**
- ⅛ **teaspoon ground nutmeg**
- ½ **cup packed brown sugar**
- ½ **cup sugar**
- 1 **cup old-fashioned oats**
- 1 **cup swirled milk chocolate and caramel chips**
- ½ **cup flaked coconut**

ADDITIONAL INGREDIENTS

- ½ **cup butter, softened**
- 1 **egg**
- ¾ **teaspoon vanilla extract**

1. In a small bowl, combine the first five ingredients. In a 1-qt. glass jar, layer flour mixture, brown sugar, sugar, oats, chips and coconut, packing well between each layer. Cover and store in a cool, dry place up to 6 months. Makes: 1 batch (4 cups).

2. To prepare cookies: Preheat oven to 350°. In a large bowl, beat butter, egg and vanilla. Add cookie mix and mix well.

3. Drop by rounded teaspoonfuls 2 in. apart onto ungreased baking sheets. Bake 9-11 minutes or until golden brown. Cool 2 minutes before removing to wire racks.

PEANUT BUTTER BROWNIE MIX

I discovered this recipe in our local newspaper, gave it a try, and my family instantly loved it. If you pack the dry ingredients in a quart canning jar, you can cover the lid with fabric for a pretty touch.

—LYNN DOWDALL PERTH, ON

PREP: 15 MIN. • **BAKE:** 25 MIN. + COOLING
MAKES: 16 BROWNIES

- 1 **cup packed brown sugar**
- ½ **cup sugar**
- ⅓ **cup baking cocoa**
- 1 **cup peanut butter chips**
- 1 **cup all-purpose flour**
- ½ **teaspoon baking powder**
- ¼ **teaspoon salt**
- ½ **cup semisweet chocolate chips**
- ½ **cup chopped walnuts**

ADDITIONAL INGREDIENTS

- 2 **eggs**
- ½ **cup butter, melted**
- 1 **teaspoon vanilla extract**

1. In a 1-qt. glass container, layer the first nine ingredients in order listed, packing well between each layer. Cover tightly. Store in a cool, dry place up to 6 months.

2. To prepare brownies: Preheat oven to 350°. In a bowl, combine eggs, butter, vanilla and brownie mix. Spread into a greased 8-in.-square baking dish. Bake 25-30 minutes or until set (do not overbake). Cool on a wire rack. Cut into squares.

Peanut Butter
Brownie Mix

OATMEAL RAISIN COOKIE MIX

You'll love the old-fashioned taste of these chewy raisin-studded cookies. I often present this as a housewarming gift or when a mom has a new baby.

—MERWYN GARBINI TUCSON, AZ

START TO FINISH: 25 MIN.
MAKES: ABOUT 5 DOZEN PER BATCH

- 1 **cup all-purpose flour**
- 1 **teaspoon baking soda**
- 1 **teaspoon ground cinnamon**
- ½ **teaspoon ground nutmeg**
- ½ **teaspoon salt**
- ¾ **cup packed brown sugar**
- ½ **cup sugar**
- ¾ **cup raisins**
- 2 **cups quick-cooking oats**

ADDITIONAL INGREDIENTS
- ¾ **cup butter, softened**
- 1 **egg**
- 1 **teaspoon vanilla extract**

1. In a bowl, combine the first five ingredients; set aside. In a 1-qt. glass container, layer brown sugar, sugar, raisins and oats, packing well between each layer. Top with reserved flour mixture. Cover and store in a cool, dry place up to 6 months. Makes: 1 batch (about 4 cups).

2. To prepare cookies: Preheat oven to 350°. In a bowl, cream butter. Beat in egg and vanilla. Add cookie mix and mix well. Drop by rounded teaspoonfuls 2 in. apart onto greased baking sheets. Bake 9-11 minutes or until golden brown. Cool 2 minutes before removing to wire racks.

PEANUT BUTTER CUP COOKIES

A cookie mix lets family and friends easily bake a batch of homemade treats whenever they have time. This one's popular because no one can resist the combination of chocolate and peanut butter!

—JUDY CRAWFORD AUXVASSE, MO

PREP: 25 MIN. • **BAKE:** 15 MIN./BATCH
MAKES: 4 DOZEN

- 1¾ cups all-purpose flour
- 1 teaspoon baking powder
- ½ teaspoon baking soda
- ¾ cup sugar
- ½ cup packed brown sugar
- 18 miniature peanut butter cups, quartered

ADDITIONAL INGREDIENTS
- ⅔ cup butter, softened
- 1 egg

1. In a small bowl, combine the flour, baking powder and baking soda. In a 1-qt. glass jar, layer the sugar, brown sugar and flour mixture; top with peanut butter cups. Cover and store in a cool, dry place for up to 1 month. Makes: 1 batch (about 4 cups total).

2. To prepare cookies: In a large bowl, beat butter and egg until well blended. Add contents of jar and stir until combined.

3. Shape dough into 1-in. balls. Place 2 in. apart on greased baking sheets (do not flatten). Bake at 375° for 12-14 minutes or until lightly browned. Remove to wire racks. Store in an airtight container.

CARAMEL OAT BAR MIX

I keep a batch of this mix on hand so I can whip up these treats in a hurry. The caramel ice cream topping and chocolate chips make them incredibly rich.

—JENNIFER JENSEN BOISE, ID

PREP: 15 MIN. • **BAKE:** 35 MIN.
MAKES: 2½ DOZEN PER BATCH

- 3 cups all-purpose flour
- 3 cups quick-cooking oats
- 1 cup packed brown sugar
- ½ cup sugar
- 3½ teaspoons baking powder
- 1 teaspoon salt
- 1½ cups shortening

ADDITIONAL INGREDIENTS
- 3 tablespoons butter, melted
- 1 cup (6 ounces) semisweet chocolate chips
- 1 jar (12 ounces) hot caramel ice cream topping

1. In a large bowl, mix the first six ingredients; cut in shortening until crumbly. Store in an airtight container in a cool, dry place up to 6 months. Makes: 2 batches (about 8 cups total).

2. To prepare bars: Preheat oven to 375°. Place 4 cups of oat mix in a bowl. Add butter; mix until blended. Reserve 1¼ cups.

3. Press remaining mixture into a greased 13x9-in. baking pan. Bake 15-17 minutes or until golden brown. Sprinkle chips over crust. Drizzle with caramel topping; carefully spread caramel to within ¼ in. of edges. Sprinkle with reserved oat mixture.

4. Bake 18-22 minutes longer or until golden brown and filling is bubbly (caramel mixture will not be set). Cool on a wire rack.

Iced Coconut
Crescents

Holiday Faves

ICED COCONUT CRESCENTS

Cookie crescents get a tropical twist when you add refreshing orange juice and coconut. Bake these goodies any time of year and decorate them to suit the season or reason.

—MARIA BENBROOK
PORT MONMOUTH, NJ

PREP: 15 MIN. • **BAKE:** 10 MIN./BATCH
MAKES: 4 DOZEN

- ½ cup butter, softened
- ¾ cup sugar
- 3 eggs
- ½ cup orange juice
- 1½ teaspoons vanilla extract
- 3 cups all-purpose flour
- 3 teaspoons baking powder
- 1⅔ cups flaked coconut

ICING
- 2 cups confectioners' sugar
- ¼ cup 2% milk
  Assorted sprinkles of your choice

1. Preheat oven to 350°. In a large bowl, cream butter and sugar until light and fluffy. Beat in eggs, orange juice and vanilla. Combine flour and baking powder; gradually add to creamed mixture and mix well. Stir in coconut.
2. Shape tablespoonfuls of dough into crescent shapes. Place 2 in. apart on ungreased baking sheets. Bake 8-10 minutes or until edges are lightly browned. Cool 1 minute before removing to wire racks to cool.
3. In a small bowl, combine the confectioners' sugar and milk. Decorate as desired with icing and sprinkles. Let stand until set.

MINT TWIST MERINGUES

Light and airy, these delicate meringues give you a refreshing burst of peppermint.
—CHERYL PERRY HERTFORD, NC

PREP: 30 MIN. • **BAKE:** 40 MIN. + STANDING
MAKES: 2 DOZEN

- 2 egg whites
- ½ teaspoon cream of tartar
- ¼ teaspoon peppermint extract
- ½ cup sugar
- ¼ cup crushed red and green mint candies

1. Place egg whites in a small bowl; let stand at room temperature 30 minutes.
2. Preheat oven to 250°. Add cream of tartar and extract to egg whites; beat on medium speed until foamy. Gradually add sugar, 1 tablespoon at a time, beating on high after each addition until sugar is dissolved. Continue beating until stiff glossy peaks form. Cut a small hole in the tip of a pastry bag or in a corner of a food-safe plastic bag; insert a small star tip. Transfer meringue to bag. Pipe 1½-in. diameter cookies 2 in. apart onto parchment paper-lined baking sheets. Sprinkle with candies.
3. Bake 40-45 minutes or until firm to the touch. Turn oven off; leave meringues in oven 1 hour. Remove from pans to a wire rack. Store in an airtight container.

CRANBERRY EGGNOG CHEESECAKE BARS

My family loves everything cheesecake. These bars combine tart cranberries and rich cream cheese, and taste even better when chilled overnight.

—CARMELL CHILDS FERRON, UT

PREP: 20 MIN.
BAKE: 50 MIN. + CHILLING
MAKES: 2 DOZEN

- 1 package spice cake mix (regular size)
- 2½ cups old-fashioned oats
- ¾ cup butter, melted
- 2 packages (8 ounces each) cream cheese, softened
- ½ cup sugar
- ⅛ teaspoon ground nutmeg
- ½ cup eggnog
- 2 tablespoons all-purpose flour
- 3 eggs
- 1 can (14 ounces) whole-berry cranberry sauce
- 2 tablespoons cornstarch

1. Preheat oven to 350°. Line a 13x9-in. baking pan with parchment paper, letting ends extend up sides; grease paper. In a large bowl, combine cake mix and oats; stir in melted butter. Reserve 1⅓ cups crumb mixture for topping; press remaining mixture onto bottom of prepared pan.

2. In a large bowl, beat cream cheese, sugar and nutmeg until smooth. Gradually beat in eggnog and flour. Add eggs; beat on low speed just until blended. Pour over crust.

3. In a small bowl, mix cranberry sauce and cornstarch until blended; spoon over cheesecake layer, spreading over top. Sprinkle with reserved crumb mixture.

4. Bake 50-55 minutes or until edges are brown and center is almost set. Cool 1 hour on a wire rack.

5. Refrigerate at least 2 hours. Lifting with parchment paper, remove from pan. Cut into bars.

NOTE *This recipe was tested with commercially prepared eggnog.*

COOKIE NOTES

_____
_____
_____
_____
_____

_____
_____
_____
_____
_____

GINGERBREAD MEN

No holiday cookie platter would be complete without gingerbread men! This is a tried-and-true recipe I'm happy to share with you.

—**MITZI SENTIFF** ANNAPOLIS, MD

PREP: 30 MIN. + CHILLING
BAKE: 10 MIN./BATCH + COOLING
MAKES: ABOUT 2 DOZEN

½ **cup butter, softened**
¾ **cup packed dark brown sugar**
⅓ **cup molasses**
1 **egg**
2 **tablespoons water**
2⅔ **cups all-purpose flour**
2 **teaspoons ground ginger**
1 **teaspoon baking soda**
½ **teaspoon salt**
½ **teaspoon each ground cinnamon, nutmeg and allspice**

1. In a large bowl, cream butter and brown sugar until light and fluffy. Beat in molasses, egg and water. Combine the flour, ginger, baking soda, salt, cinnamon, nutmeg and allspice; add to creamed mixture and mix well. Divide dough in half. Cover and refrigerate 30 minutes or until easy to handle.

2. Preheat oven to 350°. On a lightly floured surface, roll out each portion of dough to ⅛-in. thickness. Cut with a floured 4-in. cookie cutter. Place 2 in. apart on greased baking sheets. Reroll scraps.

3. Bake 8-10 minutes or until edges are firm. Remove to wire racks to cool completely. Decorate as desired.

MINTY WREATHS

You can store these in a freezer-safe container for up to three weeks, so resist the temptation to eat them all at once!

—SAMANTHA HARTZELL WASHINGTON, IL

PREP: 35 MIN. + FREEZING
BAKE: 10 MIN./BATCH
MAKES: 5 DOZEN

- ¾ **cup butter, softened**
- 1 **cup sugar**
- ⅓ **cup 2% milk**
- ¾ **teaspoon peppermint extract**
- ½ **teaspoon vanilla extract**
- 2 **cups all-purpose flour**
- ⅓ **cup baking cocoa**
- ¼ **cup cornstarch**
- ½ **teaspoon salt**
- 1 **pound dark chocolate or white candy coating, melted**
  Assorted sprinkles

1. In a large bowl, cream butter and sugar until light and fluffy. Beat in milk and extracts. Combine flour, cocoa, cornstarch and salt; gradually add to creamed mixture and mix well.

2. Shape into two 1½-in. diameter rolls; wrap each in plastic wrap. Freeze 2 hours or until firm.

3. Preheat oven to 375°. Unwrap and cut into ¼-in. slices. Place 1 in. apart on parchment paper-lined baking sheets.

4. Bake 10-12 minutes or until set. Remove to wire racks to cool completely.

5. Dip cookies in candy coating; allow excess to drip off. Place on waxed paper. Decorate as desired with sprinkles to resemble wreaths; let stand until set.

FIG & ALMOND COOKIES

In our family, holiday cookies—like these nutty fig ones—are a big deal. I'm so proud to be passing on this lovely Italian tradition to my two boys.

—ANGELA LEMOINE HOWELL, NJ

PREP: 50 MIN. + CHILLING
BAKE: 10 MIN./BATCH + COOLING
MAKES: ABOUT 6½ DOZEN

- 2 **eggs**
- 1 **tablespoon cold water**
- 2 **teaspoons vanilla extract**
- 2¾ **cups all-purpose flour**
- 1½ **cups confectioners' sugar**
- 3 **teaspoons baking powder**
- ¼ **teaspoon salt**
- 6 **tablespoons cold butter, cubed**

FILLING

- 8 **ounces dried figs (about 1⅓ cups)**
- 3 **tablespoons unblanched almonds**
- 2 **tablespoons apricot preserves**
- 4 **teaspoons orange juice**

GLAZE

- 1 **cup confectioners' sugar**
- 2 **tablespoons 2% milk**
- ½ **teaspoon vanilla extract**

1. In a small bowl, whisk eggs, cold water and vanilla until blended. Place flour, confectioners' sugar, baking powder and salt in a food processor; pulse until blended. Add butter; pulse until crumbly. While pulsing, add egg mixture just until combined.

2. Divide dough in half. Shape each into a disk; wrap in plastic wrap. Refrigerate 1 hour or until firm enough to roll.

3. Wipe food processor clean. Add figs and almonds; pulse until chopped. Add preserves and juice; pulse until combined.

4. Preheat oven to 350°. On a lightly floured surface, roll each portion of dough into a 10x8-in. rectangle; cut each lengthwise into four 2-in.-wide strips.

5. Spread about 2 tablespoons filling down center of each strip. Fold dough over filling; pinch edges to seal. Roll each gently to shape into a log; cut crosswise into 1-in. pieces.

6. Place 1 in. apart on parchment paper-lined baking sheets. Bake 10-12 minutes or until light brown. Remove from pans to wire racks to cool completely.

7. In a small bowl, mix glaze ingredients until smooth. Drizzle over cookies. Let stand until set.

LET ICING SET

When storing iced cookies, be sure to let the icing dry completely before packing them in a tin or popping them into a cookie jar.

CRANBERRY SHORTBREAD BARS

Grab a glass of milk and enjoy these bars full of cranberries, coconut and white chocolate!

—TASTE OF HOME TEST KITCHEN

PREP: 20 MIN.
BAKE: 30 MIN. + COOLING
MAKES: 2 DOZEN

- 1 cup butter, softened
- ½ cup confectioners' sugar
- 1 egg
- 1½ cups all-purpose flour
- ½ cup flaked coconut
- ⅛ teaspoon salt
- ½ cup sugar
- ½ cup packed brown sugar
- 3 tablespoons cornstarch
- 1 package (12 ounces) fresh or frozen cranberries
- 1 cup unsweetened apple juice
- 1 cup chopped walnuts
- 2 ounces white baking chocolate, melted

1. Preheat oven to 425°. In a large bowl, cream butter and confectioners' sugar until light and fluffy. Beat in egg. Combine flour, coconut and salt; gradually add to creamed mixture and mix well. Set aside 1 cup for topping. Spread remaining mixture into a greased 13x9-in. baking dish. Bake 10 minutes.

2. Meanwhile, in a small saucepan, combine sugars and cornstarch. Stir in cranberries and apple juice. Bring to a boil. Reduce heat; cook and stir 5 minutes or until thickened. Remove from heat; stir in walnuts.

3. Spread over crust. Sprinkle with reserved crumb mixture. Bake 20-25 minutes longer or until golden brown and bubbly. Cool on a wire rack. Drizzle with white chocolate. Cut into bars.

PECAN CUTOUT COOKIES

My husband's grandmother made these buttery delights with a star cutter. I've never tasted cookies quite like them—they're so nutty and flavorful.

—LOUISE REISLER BONDUEL, WI

PREP: 35 MIN.
BAKE: 10 MIN./BATCH + COOLING
MAKES: ABOUT 4 DOZEN

- 2 cups pecan halves (8 ounces)
- 1 cup sugar, divided
- 2 cups all-purpose flour
- 1 cup cold butter, cubed

VANILLA SUGAR
- ⅔ cup sugar
- ½ teaspoon vanilla extract

1. Preheat oven to 325°. Place pecans and ½ cup sugar in a food processor; process until pecans are finely ground. Transfer to a large bowl.

2. Stir flour and remaining sugar into pecan mixture; cut in butter until crumbly. Transfer mixture to a clean work surface; knead gently to form a smooth dough, about 2 minutes. (Mixture will be very crumbly at first, but will come together and form a dough as it's kneaded.) Divide dough in half.

3. On a lightly floured surface, roll each portion of dough to ¼-in. thickness. Cut with a floured 3-in. cookie cutter. Place 1 in. apart on ungreased baking sheets.

4. Bake 10-12 minutes or until edges begin to brown. Cool on pans 5 minutes. Meanwhile, in a shallow bowl, mix vanilla sugar ingredients until blended.

5. Dip warm cookies in vanilla sugar to coat; cool completely on wire racks. Store in airtight containers.

EGGNOG COOKIES

If you love eggnog, you'll be happy to find that it flavors both the cookies and the frosting in this festive recipe.
—AMANDA TAYLOR GLEN EWEN, SK

PREP: 30 MIN. + CHILLING
BAKE: 10 MIN./BATCH + COOLING
MAKES: ABOUT 13½ DOZEN

- 1 **cup butter, softened**
- 2 **cups sugar**
- 1 **cup eggnog**
- 5½ **cups all-purpose flour**
- 1 **teaspoon baking soda**
- ¾ **teaspoon ground nutmeg**

ICING
- ¼ **cup butter, softened**
- 3 **cups confectioners' sugar**
- ⅓ **cup eggnog**

1. In a large bowl, cream butter and sugar until light and fluffy. Beat in eggnog. Combine flour, baking soda and nutmeg; gradually add to creamed mixture and mix well. Shape into four 10-in. rolls; wrap each in plastic wrap. Refrigerate overnight.

2. Preheat oven to 375°. Unwrap and cut into ¼-in. slices. Place 1 in. apart on ungreased baking sheets. Bake 8-10 minutes or until set. Remove to wire racks to cool.

3. For icing, in a large bowl, beat butter until fluffy. Add confectioners' sugar and eggnog; beat until smooth. Frost cookies. Store in an airtight container.

TO MAKE AHEAD *Dough can be made 2 days in advance. Iced cookies can be stored for 1 week in an airtight container.*
NOTE *This recipe was tested with commercially prepared eggnog.*

Berry-Almond
Sandwich Cookies

BERRY-ALMOND SANDWICH COOKIES

PREP: 30 MIN. • **BAKE:** 10 MIN./BATCH + COOLING
MAKES: 3 DOZEN

1½ **cups butter, softened**
1 **cup sugar**
1 **teaspoon vanilla extract**
2¾ **cups all-purpose flour**
½ **teaspoon salt**
2 **cups ground almonds**
¾ **cup raspberry filling**
 Edible glitter or confectioners' sugar

1. Preheat oven to 325°. In a large bowl, cream butter and sugar until light and fluffy. Beat in vanilla. Combine flour and salt; gradually add to creamed mixture and mix well. Stir in almonds.
2. On a heavily floured surface, roll out dough to ⅛-in. thickness. With floured 2½-in. cookie cutters, cut into desired shapes.
3. Place 1 in. apart on ungreased baking sheets. Bake 10-12 minutes or until edges begin to brown. Remove to wire racks to cool.
4. Spread 1 teaspoon raspberry filling on the bottoms of half of the cookies; top with remaining cookies. Sprinkle with edible glitter or confectioners' sugar. Store in an airtight container.
NOTE *Edible glitter is available from Wilton Industries. Call 800-794-5866 or visit* wilton.com.

Almond shortbread cookies enclose a delightful berry filling in this irresistible Christmas favorite.

—**HELGA SCHLAPE** FLORHAM PARK, NJ

CHRUSCIKI BOW TIE COOKIES

My mother-in-law gave me the recipe for these traditional Polish "angel wings." She's been gone for years now, but we still make them in memory of her.

— LINDA & EDWARD SVERCAUSKI
SAN DIEGO, CA

PREP: 1 HOUR • **COOK:** 5 MIN./BATCH
MAKES: 4 DOZEN

- **3 egg yolks**
- **1 egg**
- **¼ cup spiced rum**
- **2 tablespoons vanilla extract**
- **½ teaspoon salt**
- **¼ cup confectioners' sugar**
- **2 cups all-purpose flour**
- **Oil for deep-fat frying**
- **Additional confectioners' sugar**

1. In a large bowl, beat the egg yolks, egg, rum, vanilla and salt until blended. Gradually add confectioners' sugar; beat until smooth. Stir in flour until a stiff dough forms. Turn onto a lightly floured surface; knead seven times.

2. Divide dough into three portions. Roll one portion into a ¼-in.-thick rectangle, about 12x5½ in. Cut in half lengthwise, then cut dough widthwise into 1½-in.-wide strips. Cut a ¾-in. lengthwise slit down the center of each strip; pull one of the ends through the slit, forming a bow. Repeat.

3. In an electric skillet or deep-fat fryer, heat oil to 375°. Fry cookies, a few at a time, for 1-2 minutes on each side or until golden brown. Drain on paper towels. Dust with confectioners' sugar.

LEMON ANGEL WINGS

The light, lemony flavor of these treats is divine. With their unique shape, they look very impressive on a cookie tray.

— CHAROLETTE WESTFALL HOUSTON, TX

PREP: 20 MIN. + CHILLING
BAKE: 20 MIN./BATCH + COOLING
MAKES: 3 DOZEN

- **1½ cups all-purpose flour**
- **1 cup cold butter, cubed**
- **½ cup sour cream**
- **1 teaspoon grated lemon peel**
- **10 tablespoons sugar, divided**

1. Place flour in a large bowl; cut in butter until crumbly. Stir in sour cream and lemon peel until well blended. Place on a piece of waxed paper; shape into a 4½-in. square. Wrap in plastic wrap and refrigerate at least 2 hours.

2. Cut dough into four 2¼-in. squares. Place one square on a piece of waxed paper sprinkled with 2 tablespoons sugar. Cover with another piece of waxed paper. Keep rest of squares refrigerated. Roll out dough into a 12x5-in. rectangle, turning often to coat both sides with sugar.

3. Lightly mark center of 12-in. side. Starting with a short side, roll up jelly-roll style to the center mark, peeling paper away while rolling. Repeat rolling from other short side, so the two rolls meet in the center and resemble a scroll.

4. Wrap in plastic wrap and refrigerate. Repeat with remaining squares, using 2 tablespoons sugar for each. Chill 1 hour.

5. Preheat oven to 375°. Unwrap dough and cut into ½-in. slices; dip each side in remaining sugar. Place 2 in. apart on foil-lined baking sheets. Bake 14 minutes or until golden brown. Turn cookies over; bake 5 minutes longer. Remove to wire racks to cool.

RASPBERRY ALMONETTES

I develop lots of original recipes. Sometimes that "missing ingredient" comes to me in my sleep, and I have to get up and jot it down. The surprising filling in these cookies—one of my favorites—makes them fun to bake and even more fun to eat!

—**ANGELA SHERIDAN** OPDYKE, IL

PREP: 55 MIN.
BAKE: 10 MIN./BATCH + COOLING
MAKES: ABOUT 3½ DOZEN

- 1 **cup butter, softened**
- 2 **cups sugar**
- 2 **eggs**
- 1 **cup canola oil**
- 2 **tablespoons almond extract**
- 4½ **cups all-purpose flour**
- 1 **teaspoon salt**
- 1 **teaspoon baking powder**
- ¾ **cup sliced almonds, finely chopped**

FILLING

- 1 **package (8 ounces) cream cheese, softened**
- ½ **cup confectioners' sugar**
- 1 **tablespoon almond extract**
- ¼ **cup red raspberry preserves**

1. Preheat oven to 350°. In a large bowl, cream butter and sugar until light and fluffy. Add eggs, one at a time, beating well after each addition. Gradually beat in oil and extract. In another bowl, whisk flour, salt and baking powder; gradually beat into creamed mixture.

2. Shape dough into 1-in. balls; press one side into almonds. Place 2 in. apart on ungreased baking sheets, almond side up. Flatten to ¼-in. thickness with bottom of a glass.

3. Bake 8-10 minutes or until edges are light brown. Cool on pans 5 minutes; remove to wire racks to cool completely.

4. For filling, in a small bowl, beat cream cheese, confectioners' sugar and extract until smooth. Place rounded teaspoonfuls of filling on bottoms of half of the cookies. Make an indentation in center of each; fill with ¼ teaspoon preserves. Cover with remaining cookies. Store in an airtight container in the refrigerator.

PEPPERMINT STICK COOKIES

PREP: 1 HOUR + CHILLING
BAKE: 10 MIN./BATCH + COOLING
MAKES: 4 DOZEN

- 1 **cup unsalted butter, softened**
- 1 **cup sugar**
- 1 **egg**
- 2 **teaspoons mint extract**
- ½ **teaspoon vanilla extract**
- 2¾ **cups all-purpose flour**
- ½ **teaspoon salt**
- 12 **drops red food coloring**
- 12 **drops green food coloring**
- 1½ **cups white baking chips**
  Crushed mint candies

1. In a large bowl, cream butter and sugar until light and fluffy. Beat in egg and extracts. Combine flour and salt; gradually add to creamed mixture and mix well.

2. Set aside half the dough. Divide remaining dough in half; add red food coloring to one portion and green food coloring to the other. Wrap dough separately in plastic wrap. Refrigerate 1-2 hours or until easy to handle.

3. Preheat oven to 350°. Divide green and red dough into 24 portions each. Divide plain dough into 48 portions.

With a cool mint flavor and a festive look, these whimsical creations will make you feel like you're at the North Pole. The chilled dough is easy to shape, too.
—**NANCY KNAPKE** FORT RECOVERY, OH

Roll each into a 4-in. rope. Place each green rope next to a white rope; press together gently and twist. Repeat with red ropes and remaining white ropes. Place 2 in. apart on ungreased baking sheets.

4. Bake 10-12 minutes or until set. Cool 2 minutes before carefully removing from pans to wire racks to cool completely.

5. In a microwave, melt white chips; stir until smooth. Dip cookie ends into melted chips; allow excess to drip off. Sprinkle with crushed candies and place on waxed paper. Let stand until set. Store in an airtight container.

CHILL OUT

You'll notice that recipes for shaped cookies, like this one, usually call for the dough to be refrigerated for a while. Letting it chill makes for easier handling and shaping of cookies later.

MERINGUE SANTA HATS

My grandkids are so excited when I make these cookies. If they come to my house, they like to put the red glitter on the meringue and love helping Grandma out.
—**BONNIE HAWKINS** ELKHORN, WI

PREP: 30 MIN.
BAKE: 40 MIN. + STANDING
MAKES: 3 DOZEN

- 2 **egg whites**
- ½ **teaspoon cream of tartar**
- ¼ **teaspoon vanilla extract**
- ½ **cup sugar**
  Red colored sugar

1. Place egg whites in a small bowl; let stand at room temperature 30 minutes.
2. Preheat oven to 250°. Add cream of tartar and vanilla to egg whites; beat on medium speed until foamy. Gradually add sugar, 1 tablespoon at a time, beating on high after each addition until sugar is dissolved. Continue beating until stiff glossy peaks form.
3. Cut a small hole in the tip of a pastry bag or in a corner of a food-safe plastic bag; insert a #8 round tip. Fill bag with one-fourth of the meringue; set aside. Prepare a second piping bag, using a #12 round tip; fill with remaining meringue.
4. Using bag with the #12 tip, pipe 36 Santa hat triangles (2 in. tall) onto parchment paper-lined baking sheets. Sprinkle with red sugar. Use first bag to pipe white trim and pom-poms on hats.
5. Bake 40-45 minutes or until firm to the touch. Turn off oven (do not open oven door); leave meringues in oven 1 hour.
6. Remove hats from paper. Store in an airtight container at room temperature.

NANNY'S FRUITCAKE COOKIES

My grandmother always made a holiday fruitcake. I took her recipe and adapted it into a cookie that's perfect any time of year with a cup of tea.

—AMANDA DIGGES SOUTH WINDSOR, CT

PREP: 35 MIN. + CHILLING
BAKE: 15 MIN./BATCH
MAKES: ABOUT 4 DOZEN

- 1⅔ cups chopped pecans or walnuts
- 1⅓ cups golden raisins
- 1 cup pitted dried plums, chopped
- ⅔ cup dried apricots, finely chopped
- ½ cup dried cranberries
- ¼ cup Triple Sec liqueur
- 1 cup butter, softened
- ½ cup sugar
- ⅓ cup packed light brown sugar
- ½ teaspoon ground nutmeg
- 1 egg
- 2⅔ cups all-purpose flour

1. Place the first five ingredients in a large bowl. Drizzle with Triple Sec and toss to combine. Let stand, covered, overnight.

2. In a large bowl, cream butter, sugars and nutmeg until light and fluffy. Beat in egg. Gradually beat in flour. Stir in fruit mixture.

3. Divide dough in half; shape each into a 12x3x1-in. rectangular log. Wrap in plastic wrap; refrigerate overnight or until firm.

4. Preheat oven to 350°. Unwrap and cut dough crosswise into ½-in. slices. Place 2 in. apart on ungreased baking sheets. Bake 13-16 minutes or until edges are light brown. Remove from pans to wire racks to cool.

VANILLA-BUTTER SUGAR COOKIES

I bake these cookies for Christmas, Valentine's Day (in heart shapes, with messages written in frosting), Thanksgiving (shaped like turkeys) and Halloween (shaped like pumpkins, of course).

—CYNTHIA ETTEL GLENCOE, MN

PREP: 35 MIN. + CHILLING
BAKE: 10 MIN./BATCH + COOLING
MAKES: 7 DOZEN (2½-IN. COOKIES)

- 1½ cups sugar
- 1½ cups butter, softened
- 2 eggs
- 2 tablespoons vanilla extract
- 4 cups all-purpose flour
- 1 teaspoon salt
- 1 teaspoon baking soda
- 1 teaspoon cream of tartar

FROSTING

- 1½ cups confectioners' sugar
- 3 tablespoons butter, softened
- 1 tablespoon vanilla extract
- 1 tablespoon milk
  Food coloring, optional
  Colored sugar

1. In a bowl, combine the sugar and butter; beat until creamy. Add eggs and vanilla; beat well. Stir together dry ingredients; gradually add to creamed mixture until completely blended. Chill for 30 minutes.

2. Preheat oven to 350°. On a lightly floured surface, roll dough to a ¼-in. thickness. Cut with holiday cutters dipped in flour. Using a floured spatula, transfer cookies to ungreased baking sheets. Bake 10-12 minutes. Cool on wire racks.

3. For frosting, combine sugar, butter, vanilla and milk; beat until creamy. Thin with additional milk to desired spreading consistency if necessary. Add a few drops of food coloring if desired. Spread frosting over cookies and decorate with colored sugar.

ANY HOLIDAY SPRINKLE COOKIES

You can roll this cookie dough in any colored sugar to suit any holiday. After you roll the dough in sugar, you can freeze the logs for up to 2 months. Just let them thaw slightly before slicing. They're easier to slice if very firm.

—LYNN MERENDINO MARYSVILLE, PA

PREP: 25 MIN. • **BAKE:** 10 MIN./BATCH
MAKES: 3 DOZEN

- ½ cup butter, softened
- 1 cup sugar
- 1 egg
- 1 tablespoon lemon juice
- 2 teaspoons vanilla extract
- 1¾ cups all-purpose flour
- ¾ teaspoon salt
- ½ teaspoon baking soda
- 1 cup flaked coconut, finely chopped
- 6 tablespoons colored sugar

1. In a small bowl, cream butter and sugar until light and fluffy. Beat in egg, lemon juice and vanilla. Combine flour, salt and baking soda; gradually add to creamed mixture and mix well. Beat in coconut.

2. Shape into two 6-in. logs; roll each in colored sugar and wrap in plastic wrap. Refrigerate 3 hours or until firm.

3. Preheat the oven to 375°. Unwrap and cut into ¼-in. slices. Place 1 in. apart on ungreased baking sheets. Bake 10-12 minutes or until set. Cool for 2 minutes before removing from pans to wire racks.

LEMON SNOWDROPS

These crunchy, buttery cookies have a puckery lemon filling. I bring them out for special gatherings.
—**BERNICE MARTINONI** PETALUMA, CA

PREP: 40 MIN. + CHILLING
BAKE: 10 MIN./BATCH + COOLING
MAKES: 2 DOZEN

- 1 **cup butter, softened**
- ½ **cup confectioners' sugar**
- ¼ **teaspoon salt**
- 1 **teaspoon lemon extract**
- 2 **cups all-purpose flour**
  Granulated sugar

FILLING
- 1 **egg, lightly beaten**
- ⅔ **cup granulated sugar**
- 3 **tablespoons lemon juice**
- 2 **teaspoons grated lemon peel**
- 4 **teaspoons butter**
  Additional confectioners' sugar

1. Preheat oven to 350°. In a bowl, cream butter, confectioners' sugar and salt until light and fluffy. Beat in extract. Gradually beat in flour. Cover and refrigerate dough until firm enough to shape.

2. Shape teaspoonfuls of dough into balls. Place 1 in. apart on ungreased baking sheets; flatten slightly with bottom of a glass dipped in sugar. Bake 10-12 minutes or until light brown. Remove from pans to wire racks to cool completely.

3. For filling, in a small heavy saucepan, whisk egg, granulated sugar, lemon juice and lemon peel until blended. Add butter; cook over medium heat, whisking constantly, until thickened and a thermometer reads at least 170°, about 20 minutes. Do not allow to boil. Remove from heat immediately. Transfer to a small bowl; cool. Press plastic wrap onto surface of filling. Refrigerate until cold, about 1 hour.

4. To serve, spread lemon filling on bottoms of half of cookies; cover with remaining cookies. Dust with confectioners' sugar. Refrigerate leftovers.

Lemon Snowdrops

WALNUT CHOCOLATE HEARTS

I've been making these cute cookies with my mom since I was a little girl. They're one of my favorites, and very fast to make.

—MARIA HULL BARTLETT, IL

PREP: 30 MIN. + CHILLING
BAKE: 10 MIN./BATCH + COOLING
MAKES: ABOUT 4 DOZEN

- 1 **cup butter, cubed**
- ⅔ **cup packed brown sugar**
- 1 **teaspoon vanilla extract**
- 1 **egg, lightly beaten**
- 2¼ **cups all-purpose flour**
- ¼ **cup baking cocoa**
- ½ **teaspoon salt**
- ¾ **cup finely chopped walnuts**

TOPPING

- 1½ **cups semisweet chocolate chips**
- 2 **tablespoons shortening**
- ½ **cup ground walnuts**

1. In a large saucepan, combine butter and brown sugar. Cook and stir over medium-low heat until butter is melted. Remove from heat; stir in vanilla. Cool 15 minutes. Stir in egg.

2. Combine flour, cocoa and salt; add to butter mixture. Fold in walnuts. Cover and chill 30 minutes or until easy to handle.

3. Preheat oven to 350°. On a lightly floured surface, roll dough to ¼-in. thickness. Cut with a floured 3-in. heart-shaped cookie cutter. Place 1 in. apart on ungreased baking sheets.

4. Bake 9-10 minutes or until edges are firm. Remove to wire racks to cool.

5. For topping, in a microwave, melt chocolate chips and shortening; stir until smooth. Dip half of each heart into chocolate mixture; allow excess to drip off. Dip edges of dipped side into ground walnuts. Place on waxed paper; let stand until set.

ITALIAN SPUMONI COOKIES

PREP: 30 MIN. + CHILLING
BAKE: 10 MIN./BATCH
MAKES: 4 DOZEN

- 2 **tubes (16½ ounces each) refrigerated sugar cookie dough**
- 1 **cup all-purpose flour, divided**
- ¼ **cup chopped maraschino cherries**
- 4 **to 6 drops red food coloring, optional**
- 2 **tablespoons baking cocoa**
- 2 **teaspoons hazelnut liqueur**
- ⅓ **cup chopped pistachios**
- 4 **to 6 drops green food coloring, optional**

1. Let cookie dough stand at room temperature 5-10 minutes to soften. In a large bowl, beat cookie dough and ¾ cup flour until combined. Divide dough into three portions.

2. Add remaining flour, cherries and, if desired, red food coloring to one portion. Add cocoa and liqueur to the second portion. Add pistachios and, if desired, green food coloring to the remaining portion.

3. Roll each portion between two pieces of waxed paper into an 8x6-in. rectangle. Remove waxed paper. Place cherry rectangle on a piece of plastic wrap. Layer with chocolate and pistachio rectangles; press together lightly. Wrap with plastic wrap and refrigerate overnight.

4. Preheat oven to 375°. Cut chilled dough in half widthwise. Return one rectangle to the refrigerator. Cut remaining rectangle into ¼-in. slices. Place 1 in. apart on ungreased baking sheets. Repeat with remaining dough.

5. Bake 8-10 minutes or until set. Cool 2 minutes before removing to wire racks. Store in an airtight container.

Folks will think you made these from scratch, but refrigerated cookie dough makes them a cinch to bake. We'll never tell your secret!
—TASTE OF HOME TEST KITCHEN

COOKIE NOTES

APRICOT-FILLED SANDWICH COOKIES

When I bring a tray of homemade treats to school or Christmas parties, these pretty cookies are always the first to disappear! People have even asked me to make them for wedding receptions.

—DEB LYON BANGOR, PA

PREP: 40 MIN.
BAKE: 10 MIN./BATCH +COOLING
MAKES: 4 DOZEN

- 1 **cup butter, softened**
- 1 **cup sugar**
- 2 **eggs**
- 3 **cups all-purpose flour**
- ⅔ **cup finely chopped walnuts**

FILLING
- 2 **cups dried apricots**
- ¾ **cup water**
- ¼ **cup sugar**
- ½ **teaspoon ground cinnamon**

TOPPING
- ½ **cup semisweet chocolate chips**
- ½ **teaspoon shortening**
- 4 **teaspoons confectioners' sugar**

1. Preheat oven to 350°. In a large bowl, cream butter and sugar until light and fluffy. Beat in eggs. Combine flour and walnuts; gradually add to creamed mixture and mix well.

2. Shape into 1½-in.-thick logs. Cut into ¼-in. slices. Place 2 in. apart on ungreased baking sheets.

3. Bake 10-12 minutes or until bottoms begin to brown. Cool completely on pans on wire racks.

4. Meanwhile, in a large saucepan, combine apricots and water. Bring to a boil. Cook and stir 10 minutes or until apricots are tender. Drain and cool to room temperature.

5. In a blender or food processor, combine the sugar, cinnamon and apricots. Cover and process until smooth. Spread over bottoms of half of the cookies; top with remaining cookies.

6. For topping, melt chocolate chips and shortening; stir until smooth. Drizzle over cookies. Sprinkle with confectioners' sugar.

FAVORITE SUGAR COOKIES

Making these cookies is a family tradition. Have fun decorating them together!
—**JUDITH SCHOLOVICH** WAUKESHA, WI

PREP: 30 MIN. + CHILLING
BAKE: 10 MIN./BATCH + COOLING
MAKES: 6-7 DOZEN

- 1 **cup butter, softened**
- 1 **cup confectioners' sugar**
- 1 **egg**
- 1½ **teaspoons almond extract**
- 1 **teaspoon vanilla extract**
- 2½ **cups all-purpose flour**
- 1 **teaspoon salt**

FROSTING

- 6 **tablespoons butter, softened**
- 3 **cups confectioners' sugar**
- 1 **teaspoon vanilla extract**
- 2 **to 4 tablespoons 2% milk**
  Food coloring of your choice, optional

Colored sugar, edible glitter, nonpareils or frosting of your choice, optional

1. In a large bowl, cream butter and confectioners' sugar until light and fluffy. Beat in egg and extracts. Combine flour and salt; add to creamed mixture and mix well. Chill 1-2 hours.

2. Preheat oven to 375°. On a lightly floured surface, roll dough to 1/8-in. thickness. Cut with floured 2½-in. cookie cutters. Place on greased baking sheets. Bake 7-9 minutes or until lightly browned. Remove to wire racks to cool.

3. For frosting, in a small bowl, combine butter, sugar, vanilla and enough milk to achieve a spreading consistency. If desired, tint with food coloring. Frost cookies; decorate as desired.

RASPBERRY LINZER COOKIES

These wonderful cookies require a bit of extra effort to make and assemble, but the delight on the faces of family and friends when I serve them makes it all worthwhile.

—SCHELBY THOMPSON

CAMDEN WYOMING, DE

PREP: 30 MIN. + CHILLING
BAKE: 10 MIN./BATCH + COOLING
MAKES: 2 DOZEN

- 1   cup butter, softened
- 1¼ cups sugar, divided
- 2   eggs, separated
- 2½ cups all-purpose flour
- ¼   teaspoon salt

Confectioners' sugar
- ½   cup ground almonds
- ¾   cup raspberry preserves

1. In a large bowl, cream butter. Gradually add ⅔ cup sugar, beating until light and fluffy. Add egg yolks, one at a time, beating well after each addition. Combine flour and salt; gradually add to creamed mixture and mix well. Shape dough into a ball; cover and refrigerate 30-45 minutes or until firm.

2. Preheat oven to 350°. On a surface dusted with confectioners' sugar, roll half of the dough to ⅛-in. thickness; cut with a floured 2½-in. round cookie cutter. Repeat with remaining dough, using a floured 2½-in. doughnut cutter so the center is cut out of each cookie.

3. Beat egg whites until frothy. Combine almonds and remaining sugar. Brush each cookie with egg white and sprinkle with the almond mixture. Place on greased baking sheets. Bake 6-8 minutes or until lightly browned. Remove to wire racks to cool completely.

4. Spread 2 teaspoons of raspberry preserves over the plain side of solid cookies. Place cookies with centers cut out, almond side up, on top of the preserves, making a sandwich.

COOKIE NOTES

HONEY-NUT CHRISTMAS COOKIES

My sons, Aaron and Zach, can't wait for these cookies at Christmastime. They like to warm them in the microwave. These special sweets are well worth the time they take.
—**GLENDA HERZ** LAWRENCE, NE

PREP: 30 MIN. • **BAKE:** 20 MIN./BATCH
MAKES: ABOUT 3½ DOZEN

- 2 **cups all-purpose flour**
- 1 **cup cold butter, cubed**
- 1 **package (8 ounces) cream cheese, softened**
- ¼ **cup sugar**
- 1½ **cups chopped pecans, divided**
- ⅓ **cup plus ¼ cup honey, divided**
- 1 **teaspoon butter, melted**
- ½ **teaspoon ground cinnamon**

1. Place flour in a large bowl. Cut in cold butter and cream cheese until mixture resembles coarse crumbs.

Shape into two disks; wrap in plastic wrap. Refrigerate for 2 hours or until easy to handle.

2. Preheat oven to 325°. Place sugar and 1 cup pecans in a food processor; cover and process until pecans are finely chopped. Transfer to a small bowl; stir in ⅓ cup honey, melted butter and cinnamon.

3. On a lightly floured surface, roll one portion of dough to ⅛-in. thickness. Cut with a floured 2-in. round cookie cutter. Place a teaspoonful of filling on the center of half of the circles; top with remaining circles. Press edges with a fork to seal. Repeat with remaining dough.

4. Transfer to greased baking sheets. Brush with remaining honey and sprinkle with remaining pecans. Bake 18-22 minutes or until golden brown. Remove to wire racks to cool.

TO MAKE AHEAD *Baked cookies can be frozen for up to 1 month.*

Spiced German
Cookies

SPICED GERMAN COOKIES

It wouldn't be Christmas in our house without these. They're the perfect cross between a sugar cookie and a perfectly spiced gingerbread cookie.
—**APRIL DRASIN** VAN NUYS, CA

PREP: 30 MIN. + CHILLING
BAKE: 10 MIN./BATCH
MAKES: 5 DOZEN

- 1 **cup butter, softened**
- 1 **cup sugar**
- 2 **eggs**
- 2 **teaspoons vanilla extract**
- 1 **teaspoon lemon extract**
- 3½ **cups all-purpose flour**
- 2 **teaspoons baking powder**
- 1 **teaspoon each ground cardamom, coriander, cinnamon and cloves**
- ½ **teaspoon salt**
- ¾ **cup slivered almonds**

1. In a large bowl, cream butter and sugar until light and fluffy. Beat in eggs and extracts. In another bowl, whisk flour, baking powder, spices and salt; gradually beat into creamed mixture.
2. Divide dough in half. Shape each into a disk; wrap in plastic wrap. Refrigerate 1 hour or until firm enough to roll.
3. Preheat oven to 350°. On a lightly floured surface, roll each portion of dough to ⅛-in. thickness. Cut with floured 3-in. holiday cookie cutters. Place 1 in. apart on ungreased baking sheets. Decorate tops with almonds, pressing to adhere.
4. Bake 9-11 minutes or until light brown. Remove from pans to wire racks to cool. Store in airtight containers.

CREAM CHEESE DAINTIES

The cream cheese makes these tender treats just melt in your mouth.
—**LYNNE STEWART** JULIAN, PA

PREP: 20 MIN. + CHILLING
BAKE: 15 MIN./BATCH
MAKES: 4 DOZEN

- 1 **cup butter, softened**
- 1 **package (8 ounces) cream cheese, softened**
- 2½ **cups all-purpose flour**
- ½ **cup apricot spreadable fruit or seedless raspberry preserves**

1. In a large bowl, cream butter and cream cheese until light and fluffy. Gradually add flour to the creamed mixture and mix well. Divide dough into four portions; cover and refrigerate until easy to handle.
2. On a lightly floured surface, roll one portion of dough at a time into a 10x7½-in. rectangle. Trim edges if necessary. Cut into 2½-in. squares.
3. Place ¼ teaspoon spreadable fruit or preserves near each end of two diagonal corners. Moisten the remaining two corners with water; fold over and press lightly.
4. Place on ungreased baking sheets. Bake at 350° for 12-15 minutes or until corners are lightly browned. Cool 2-3 minutes before removing to wire racks to cool.

CARAMEL-WALNUT STAR COOKIES

These crisp, buttery stars will shine brightly on any dessert tray. The first time I tried them was at a potluck, and I spent the rest of the evening tracking down the recipe!

—SANDY TOPALOF NORTH ROYALTON, OH

PREP: 30 MIN.
BAKE: 15 MIN./BATCH + CHILLING
MAKES: 2 DOZEN

- 1½ **cups all-purpose flour**
- ⅓ **cup sugar**
- ½ **cup cold butter**
- 2 **tablespoons 2% milk**
- ½ **teaspoon vanilla extract**
- ½ **cup chopped walnuts, toasted**
- 24 **walnut halves**
- ⅔ **cup semisweet chocolate chips, melted**

GLAZE

- ¼ **cup packed brown sugar**
- 2 **tablespoons butter, cubed**
- 1 **tablespoon 2% milk**
- ⅓ **cup confectioners' sugar**

1. Preheat oven to 350°. In a small bowl, combine flour and sugar. Cut in butter until the mixture resembles coarse crumbs. Stir in milk and vanilla, then chopped walnuts.

2. On a lightly floured surface, roll out dough to ¼-in. thickness. Cut with a 3-in. star-shaped cookie cutter dipped in flour. Place 2 in. apart on greased baking sheets. Press a walnut half in the center of each. Bake 12-15 minutes or until edges are lightly browned. Remove to wire racks to cool.

3. Spread bottoms of cookies with melted chocolate. Place chocolate side up on waxed paper-lined baking sheets. Refrigerate until set.

4. For glaze, in a small saucepan, bring brown sugar and butter to a boil. Cook and stir 30 seconds. Remove from the heat; cool 5 minutes. Whisk in milk until smooth. Stir in confectioners' sugar. Immediately drizzle over top of cookies. Let stand until set.

TO MAKE AHEAD *Dough can be made 2 days in advance. Iced cookies can be stored 1 week in an airtight container at room temperature or frozen up to 1 month.*

HAZELNUT ESPRESSO FINGERS IN CHOCOLATE

I give these cookies out to teachers and staff around Christmas and at the end of the school year. They're also in high demand at bake sales.

—CINDY BEBERMAN ORLAND PARK, IL

PREP: 35 MIN.
BAKE: 10 MIN./BATCH + COOLING
MAKES: 5 DOZEN

- 1½ cups hazelnuts, toasted
- 1 cup butter, softened
- ⅔ cup sugar
- 1 tablespoon instant espresso powder
- 2 teaspoons vanilla extract
- 2 cups all-purpose flour
- ½ teaspoon salt
- ¾ cup milk chocolate chips
- ¾ cup semisweet chocolate chips
- 2 teaspoons shortening

1. Preheat oven to 350°. Place the hazelnuts in a food processor; cover and process until ground. Set aside. In a large bowl, cream butter and sugar until light and fluffy. Beat in espresso powder and vanilla. Combine flour and salt; gradually add to creamed mixture and mix well. Stir in hazelnuts.

2. Shape scant tablespoonfuls of dough into 2-in. logs. Place 2 in. apart on ungreased baking sheets. Bake 9-11 minutes or until edges are lightly browned. Remove to wire racks to cool completely.

3. In a microwave, melt chocolate chips and shortening; stir until smooth. Dip each cookie halfway into chocolate mixture, allowing excess to drip off. Place on waxed paper; let stand until set. Store in an airtight container.

COFFEE BONBONS

When I first sampled this confection, I decided it was the best cookie I'd ever tasted! The coffee flavor and chocolate icing make it a delightful treat.

—LEITZEL MALZAHN FOX POINT, WI

PREP: 20 MIN.
BAKE: 20 MIN./BATCH + COOLING
MAKES: 5 DOZEN

- 1 cup butter, softened
- ¾ cup confectioners' sugar
- ½ teaspoon vanilla extract
- 1 tablespoon instant coffee granules
- 1¾ cups all-purpose flour

CHOCOLATE GLAZE
- 1 tablespoon butter
- ½ ounce unsweetened chocolate
- 1 cup confectioners' sugar
- 2 tablespoons milk

1. In a bowl, cream butter and sugar until light and fluffy. Add vanilla. Combine coffee and flour; stir into creamed mixture and mix well. Chill. Shape into ¾-in. balls and place on ungreased baking sheets. Bake at 350° for 18-20 minutes.

2. Meanwhile, for glaze, melt butter and chocolate together. Add melted mixture to sugar, along with milk; beat until smooth. Frost cookies while still warm.

SANTA CLAUS SUGAR COOKIES

My mom taught me how to make these tender, buttery Santa cookies and hang them on the tree. Her tradition has lasted 40 years and counting.

—ANN BUSH COLORADO CITY, CO

PREP: 45 MIN. + CHILLING
BAKE: 10 MIN./BATCH + COOLING
MAKES: 4 DOZEN

- 1 **cup unsalted butter**
- 1½ **cups sugar**
- 2 **eggs**
- 1 **teaspoon vanilla extract**
- 3½ **cups all-purpose flour**
- 1 **teaspoon baking soda**
- 1 **teaspoon cream of tartar**
- ½ **teaspoon ground nutmeg**
- ¼ **teaspoon salt**

FROSTING

- ¾ **cup unsalted butter, softened**
- 6 **tablespoons 2% milk**
- 2¼ **teaspoons vanilla extract**
- ¼ **teaspoon salt**
- 6¾ **cups confectioners' sugar**
  Optional decorations: red colored sugar, miniature semisweet chocolate chips and Red Hots

1. In a large bowl, cream butter and sugar until light and fluffy. Beat in eggs and vanilla. In another bowl, whisk flour, baking soda, cream of tartar, nutmeg and salt; gradually beat into creamed mixture.

2. Divide dough in half. Shape each into a disk; wrap in plastic wrap. Refrigerate 1 hour or until firm enough to roll.

3. Preheat oven to 375°. On a lightly floured surface, roll each portion of dough to ¼-in. thickness. Cut with a floured 3-in. Santa-shaped cookie cutter. Place 2 in. apart on greased baking sheets.

4. Bake 8-10 minutes or until light brown. Remove from pans to wire racks to cool completely.

5. For frosting, in a large bowl, beat butter until creamy. Beat in milk, vanilla and salt. Gradually beat in confectioners' sugar until smooth. Pipe onto cookies and decorate as desired.

STACKED CHRISTMAS TREE COOKIES

Using prepared cookie dough gives you a head start on this little forest of Christmas trees. Add or subtract cookies to vary the height of the trees.

—SUE DRAHEIM WATERFORD, WI

PREP: 30 MIN.
BAKE: 10 MIN. + COOLING
MAKES: 9 COOKIES

- 1 tube (16½ ounces) refrigerated sugar cookie dough
- ½ teaspoon vanilla extract
- ½ cup all-purpose flour
  Green colored sugar and red nonpareils
- 1 can (16 ounces) vanilla frosting
- 9 wrapped Rolo candies
  Gumdrops, halved crosswise
- 9 peppermint candies
  Water

1. Preheat oven to 350°. Place cookie dough in a large bowl; let stand at room temperature 5-10 minutes to soften.

Beat in vanilla. Add flour; beat until blended.

2. On a lightly floured surface, roll dough to ¼-in. thickness. Using a floured 2-in. round cookie cutter, cut out 18 cookies. Repeat with 1½-in. and 1-in. round cookie cutters.

3. Sprinkle cookies with colored sugar; decorate edges with nonpareils. Place 1 in. apart on ungreased baking sheets. Bake 6-9 minutes or until edges are light brown. Remove to wire racks to cool completely. For each Christmas tree, pipe frosting on top of a Rolo candy for a trunk; top with a 2-in. cookie. Pipe frosting on top and bottom of a gumdrop; place in center of cookie. Top with another 2-in. cookie. Repeat layers with two 1½-in. cookies and two 1-in. cookies, piping frosting on gumdrops to adhere layers.

4. Attach a peppermint candy to the top using additional frosting. Thin remaining frosting with water; drizzle over edges.

Buttery Spritz
Cookies

BUTTERY SPRITZ COOKIES

These little gems always remind people of the holidays. The dough is easy to work with, so it's fun to make these into a variety of festive shapes for holidays and other occasions.

—BEVERLY LAUNIUS SANDWICH, IL

PREP: 20 MIN. • **BAKE:** 10 MIN./BATCH
MAKES: 7½ DOZEN

- 1 **cup butter, softened**
- 1¼ **cups confectioners' sugar**
- 1 **egg**
- 1 **teaspoon vanilla extract**
- ½ **teaspoon almond extract**
- 2½ **cups all-purpose flour**
- ½ **teaspoon salt**
  Melted chocolate candy coating, optional
  Colored sugar and sprinkles, optional

1. Preheat oven to 375°. In a large bowl, cream butter and confectioners' sugar until light and fluffy. Beat in egg and extracts. Combine flour and salt. Gradually add to creamed mixture; mix well.

2. Using a cookie press fitted with the disk of your choice, press dough 2 in. apart onto ungreased baking sheets. If desired, decorate with colored sugar and sprinkles.

3. Bake 6-8 minutes or until set (do not brown). Remove to wire racks to cool completely. If desired, dip baked cookies in melted candy coating and decorate with sprinkles. Let stand until set.

COOKIE NOTES

_____
_____
_____
_____
_____
_____
_____
_____
_____
_____
_____
_____
_____
_____
_____
_____
_____
_____
_____
_____
_____
_____
_____
_____
_____
_____
_____
_____
_____
_____
_____
_____
_____
_____
_____
_____
_____
_____

ALMOND BONBON COOKIES

Almond paste is wrapped in cookie dough for these bite-sized treats. Dip cooled cookies into one frosting or dip each side into different flavors of frosting. Get creative with sprinkle toppings!

—**TERI RASEY** CADILLAC, MI

PREP: 20 MIN. • **BAKE:** 10 MIN./BATCH
MAKES: 4 DOZEN

- 1 **cup butter, softened**
- ⅔ **cup confectioners' sugar**
- ¼ **cup 2% milk**
- 1 **teaspoon vanilla extract**
- 3 **cups all-purpose flour**
- 1 **package (7 ounces) almond paste**

VANILLA ICING
- 1 **cup confectioners' sugar**
- 4½ **teaspoons 2% milk**
- 1 **teaspoon vanilla extract**

CHOCOLATE ICING
- 1 **cup confectioners' sugar**
- 1 **ounce unsweetened chocolate, melted and cooled**
- 3 **tablespoons 2% milk**

- 1 **teaspoon vanilla extract**
  Assorted sprinkles

1. Preheat oven to 375°. In a large bowl, cream butter and confectioners' sugar until light and fluffy. Beat in milk and vanilla. Gradually beat in flour.

2. Cut almond paste into 12 slices (about ¼ in. thick); cut each into quarters. Shape into balls. Wrap tablespoons of cookie dough around almond paste to cover completely. Place 2 in. apart on ungreased baking sheets.

3. Bake 10-12 minutes or until golden brown. Remove to wire racks to cool completely.

4. In a small bowl, mix vanilla icing ingredients until smooth. For chocolate icing, mix confectioners' sugar, cooled chocolate, milk and vanilla until smooth. Dip cookies in icings as desired; allow excess to drip off. Decorate with sprinkles. Place on waxed paper; let stand until set. Store in airtight containers.

JOLLY GINGER REINDEER COOKIES

I made gingerbread cookies for years before realizing my gingerbread-man cutter becomes a reindeer when turned upside down. These cookies are festive and wonderfully fun.

—SUE GRONHOLZ BEAVER DAM, WI

PREP: 50 MIN. + CHILLING
BAKE: 10 MIN./BATCH + COOLING
MAKES: ABOUT 4 DOZEN

- ½ cup butter, softened
- 1 cup packed brown sugar
- 1 egg
- ¾ cup molasses
- 3½ cups all-purpose flour
- 2 teaspoons ground ginger
- 1 teaspoon baking powder
- 1 teaspoon baking soda
- 1 teaspoon ground cinnamon
- 1 teaspoon ground allspice

ROYAL ICING

- 2 cups confectioners' sugar
- 2 tablespoons plus 2 teaspoons water
- 4 teaspoons meringue powder
- ¼ teaspoon cream of tartar
- 1 to 2 tablespoons miniature semisweet chocolate chips
- 1 to 2 tablespoons Red Hots

1. In a large bowl, cream butter and brown sugar until light and fluffy. Beat in egg and molasses. In another bowl, whisk flour, ginger, baking powder, baking soda, cinnamon and allspice; gradually beat into creamed mixture.

2. Divide dough in half. Shape each into a disk; wrap in plastic wrap. Refrigerate 1 hour or until firm enough to roll.

3. Preheat oven to 350°. On a lightly floured surface, roll each portion of dough to ¼-in. thickness. Cut with a floured 3-in. gingerbread boy-shaped cookie cutter. Place 1 in. apart on greased baking sheets.

4. Bake 10-12 minutes or until set. Cool on pans 1 minute. Remove to wire racks to cool completely.

5. In a bowl, combine confectioners' sugar, water, meringue powder and cream of tartar; beat on low speed just until blended. Beat on high 4-5 minutes or until stiff peaks form. Keep unused icing covered at all times with a damp cloth. If necessary, beat again on high speed to restore texture.

6. To decorate the cookies, place gingerbread boys on a work surface with heads facing you. Pipe antlers onto legs. With icing, attach chocolate chips for eyes and Red Hots for noses. Let stand until set. Store in airtight containers.

General Index

ALMOND PASTE
ALMOND BONBON COOKIES..........202
ALMOND-BUTTER COOKIE
    BOUQUET..........................97

ALMONDS
ALMOND APRICOT BARS 144
BERRY-ALMOND SANDWICH
    COOKIES.........................179
CHOCOLATE ALMOND CRESCENTS 66
CHOCOLATE-DIPPED ALMOND
    MACAROONS.......................69
CHOCOLATE-DIPPED ANISE
    BISCOTTI.........................27
FIG & ALMOND COOKIES..............175
RASPBERRY ALMONETTES.............181
SUGAR DOVES.........................93
VANILLA CRESCENTS 53

ANISE
ANISE BUTTER COOKIES................36
CHOCOLATE-DIPPED ANISE
    BISCOTTI.........................27

APPLES
APPLE CARAMEL CHEESECAKE BARS ..131

APRICOTS
ALMOND APRICOT BARS 144
APRICOT-FILLED SANDWICH
    COOKIES.........................190
THUMBPRINT BUTTER COOKIES........23
VIENNESE COOKIES.....................46

BANANAS
FROSTED BANANA BARS...............117

BARS (also see Blondies; Brownies)
ALMOND APRICOT BARS 144
ALMOST A CANDY BAR 114
APPLE CARAMEL CHEESECAKE BARS ..131
BLACKBERRY CHEESECAKE BARS......132
BLUEBERRY CRUMB BARS.............150
CALGARY NANAIMO BARS 122
CARAMEL OAT BAR MIX...............169
CHERRY BARS.......................148
CHERRY WALNUT SQUARES............149
CHEWY CHOCOLATE-CHERRY BARS..113
CHEWY HONEY GRANOLA BARS 113
CHOCOLATE-PEANUT BUTTER
    CRUNCH BARS 136
CHOCOLATE PECAN PIE BARS.........142
CHOCOLATE TOFFEE DELIGHTS.......123
CINNAMON NUT BARS................152
COCONUT CHIP NUT BARS............125
COCONUT CITRUS BARS..............126
CRANBERRY EGGNOG CHEESECAKE
    BARS 172
CRANBERRY SHORTBREAD BARS 176
CRISPY STAR POPS....................83
FROSTED BANANA BARS..............117
HALLOWEEN PUMPKIN BARS..........109
HONEY-PECAN SQUARES..............118
KEY LIME BARS.....................135
LAYERED GINGERBREAD BARS.........140
MACADAMIA LEMON BARS 143
MIX FOR CRANBERRY LEMONADE
    BARS 158
PEANUT BUTTER CAKE BARS 121

PEANUT BUTTER CRISPY BARS........126
PEANUT BUTTER SQUARES............139
PUMPKIN BARS WITH BROWNED
    BUTTER FROSTING................145
PUMPKIN CREAM CHEESE BARS 139
RASPBERRY BARS....................131
RICH BUTTERSCOTCH BARS...........118
TOFFEE CHEESECAKE BARS 155
WARREN'S OATMEAL JAM SQUARES ..134
YUMMY COOKIE BARS 146

BISCOTTI (see Cookies, Shaped)

BLACKBERRIES
BLACKBERRY CHEESECAKE BARS......132

BLONDIES
(also see Bars; Brownies)
CHUNKY BLOND BROWNIES...........128
WHITE BROWNIES....................148

BLUEBERRIES
BLUEBERRY CRUMB BARS.............150

BROWNIES
(also see Bars; Blondies)
BASIC BROWNIE MIX.................162
CAPPUCCINO BROWNIES..............154
CARAMEL TOFFEE BROWNIES.........153
CHOCOLATE MINT BROWNIES.........129
CHOCOLATE SAUCE BROWNIES.......119
COBBLESTONE BROWNIES............121
COOKIE DOUGH BROWNIES...........130
CREAM CHEESE SWIRL BROWNIES ...115
DIPPED BROWNIE POPS 100
GERMAN CHOCOLATE BROWNIES 120
GOLD RUSH BROWNIES 135
PEANUT BUTTER BROWNIE MIX......166
PEANUT BUTTER-HAZELNUT
    BROWNIES.......................138
PEPPERMINT-FUDGE BROWNIE MIX ..163
RASPBERRY TRUFFLE BROWNIES......147
SAND ART BROWNIE MIX 158
TRIPLE-LAYER PRETZEL BROWNIES....122
ULTIMATE DOUBLE CHOCOLATE
    BROWNIES.......................127

BUTTERSCOTCH
ALMOST A CANDY BAR 114
BUTTERSCOTCH TOFFEE COOKIES......9
RICH BUTTERSCOTCH BARS...........118

CARAMEL
APPLE CARAMEL CHEESECAKE
    BARS 131
BASIC BROWNIE MIX.................162
CARAMEL APPLE COOKIES.............104
CARAMEL OAT BAR MIX...............169
CARAMEL TOFFEE BROWNIES.........153
CARAMEL-WALNUT STAR COOKIES....196
DOUBLE-DRIZZLE PECAN COOKIES.....40
SALTED CASHEW & CARAMEL
    CHEWS...........................80

CASHEWS
EXTRA-SPECIAL CASHEW
    CRESCENTS.......................41
SALTED CASHEW & CARAMEL
    CHEWS...........................80

CHERRIES
BASIC BROWNIE MIX.................162
CHERRY BARS.......................148
CHERRY BONBON COOKIES 19
CHERRY-NUT COOKIES 26
CHERRY WALNUT SQUARES...........149
CHEWY CHOCOLATE-CHERRY
    BARS...........................113
ITALIAN SPUMONI COOKIES..........189
LIME SHORTBREAD WITH DRIED
    CHERRIES........................62

CHOCOLATE
(also see White Chips)
BARS
ALMOST A CANDY BAR 114
CALGARY NANAIMO BARS 122
CARAMEL OAT BAR MIX...............169
CHEWY CHOCOLATE-CHERRY BARS...113
CHOCOLATE-PEANUT BUTTER
    CRUNCH BARS 136
COCONUT CHIP NUT BARS............125
PEANUT BUTTER CAKE BARS 121
PEANUT BUTTER SQUARES............139
TOFFEE CHEESECAKE BARS 155
YUMMY COOKIE BARS 146

BLONDIES
CHUNKY BLOND BROWNIES...........128

BROWNIES
BASIC BROWNIE MIX.................162
CAPPUCCINO BROWNIES..............154
CHOCOLATE MINT BROWNIES.........129
CHOCOLATE SAUCE BROWNIES.......119
COBBLESTONE BROWNIES............121
COOKIE DOUGH BROWNIES...........130
CREAM CHEESE SWIRL BROWNIES ...115
DIPPED BROWNIE POPS 100
GERMAN CHOCOLATE BROWNIES 120
GOLD RUSH BROWNIES 135
PEANUT BUTTER BROWNIE MIX......166
PEANUT BUTTER-HAZELNUT
    BROWNIES.......................138
PEPPERMINT-FUDGE BROWNIE MIX ..163
RASPBERRY TRUFFLE BROWNIES......147
SAND ART BROWNIE MIX 158
TRIPLE-LAYER PRETZEL BROWNIES....122
ULTIMATE DOUBLE CHOCOLATE
    BROWNIES.......................127

COOKIES
CHIPOTLE CRACKLE COOKIES..........81
CHOCOLATE ALMOND CRESCENTS 66
CHOCOLATE CHAI SNICKERDOODLES. .65
CHOCOLATE CHIP COOKIE MIX.......159
CHOCOLATE-DIPPED ALMOND
    MACAROONS.......................69
CHOCOLATE-DIPPED ANISE BISCOTTI..27
CHOCOLATE-DIPPED ORANGE SPRITZ. .55
CHOCOLATE-DIPPED STRAWBERRY
    MERINGUE ROSES..................99
CHOCOLATE MEXICAN WEDDING
    CAKES...........................56
CHOCOLATE ORANGE
    CHECKERBOARD COOKIES...........16
CHOCOLATE-PEANUT BUTTER CUP
    COOKIES.........................32
CHOCOLATE PECAN PIE BARS.........142

CHOCOLATE PRETZELS................49
CHOCOLATE REINDEER................94
CHOCOLATE SANDWICH COOKIES....37
CHOCOLATE TOFFEE DELIGHTS.......123
CHRISTMAS MICE COOKIES...........108
COFFEE BONBONS 197
COWBOY COOKIE MIX................157
CRANBERRY-CHOCOLATE CHIP
   COOKIE MIX........................164
DOUBLE-DRIZZLE PECAN COOKIES.....40
FROSTED MALTED MILK COOKIES......25
FUDGE-FILLED SANDIES................77
FUDGE-FILLED TOFFEE COOKIES 33
GIANT MONSTER COOKIES 51
HAZELNUT CHOCOLATE CHIP
   PIZZELLE 68
HEDGEHOG COOKIES..................106
HOMEMADE MACAROON KISSES.......70
ITALIAN SPUMONI COOKIES 189
JUMBO CHOCOLATE CHIP COOKIES ...13
LOADED-UP PRETZEL COOKIES.........15
MINTY WREATHS 174
MY KIDS' FAVORITE COOKIES 19
NORWEGIAN CHOCOLATE CHIP
   COOKIES 57
OATMEAL CHIP COOKIES...............53
OWL COOKIES........................110
PEANUT BUTTER CUP COOKIES 169
PEANUT CHOCOLATE WHIRLS 20
PISTACHIO CHOCOLATE MACARONS ...14
QUADRUPLE CHOCOLATE CHUNK
   COOKIES 10
RED VELVET WHOOPIE PIES 64
SALTED CASHEW & CARAMEL
   CHEWS.............................80
SCALLOPED MOCHA COOKIES 50
SECRET KISS COOKIES 81
SPICY OATMEAL COOKIE MIX.........166
STRAWBERRY VALENTINE COOKIES ...86
TOM TURKEYS 101
TRIPLE-CHOCOLATE BROWNIE
   COOKIES 62
TRIPLE CHOCOLATE COOKIE MIX 157
TRUFFLE-FILLED COOKIE TARTS.......58
VIENNESE COOKIES....................46
WALNUT CHOCOLATE HEARTS 188

CINNAMON
CINNAMON NUT BARS.................152

COCONUT
ANY HOLIDAY SPRINKLE COOKIES....185
CALGARY NANAIMO BARS 122
COBBLESTONE BROWNIES 121
COCONUT CHIP NUT BARS 125
COCONUT CITRUS BARS...............126
COCONUT CLOUDS....................18
COCONUT DROP COOKIES 29
COCONUT RASPBERRY COOKIES 45
GERMAN CHOCOLATE BROWNIES 120
HOMEMADE MACAROON KISSES.......70
ICED COCONUT CRESCENTS 171
LOADED-UP PRETZEL COOKIES.........15
MY KIDS' FAVORITE COOKIES 19
RANGER COOKIES 26
RASPBERRY BARS 131

COFFEE
CAPPUCCINO BROWNIES..............154
COFFEE BONBONS 197
HAZELNUT ESPRESSO FINGERS IN
   CHOCOLATE 197
SCALLOPED MOCHA COOKIES 50

COOKIES
(also see Bars; Blondies; Brownies)
CUTOUT COOKIES
ALMOND-BUTTER COOKIE
   BOUQUET...........................97
ANISE BUTTER COOKIES................36
CARAMEL-WALNUT STAR COOKIES....196
CRISP SUGAR COOKIE MIX 161
ELF COOKIES.........................103
EXTRA-SPECIAL CASHEW
   CRESCENTS 41
FAVORITE SUGAR COOKIES...........191
FOLDED HAZELNUT COOKIES 48
FROSTED MALTED MILK COOKIES......25
GIANT DINOSAUR COOKIES............83
GINGERBREAD MEN...................173
GINGERBREAD SKELETONS.............88
GLAZED MAPLE SHORTBREAD
   COOKIES 22
HALLOWEEN CUTOUT COOKIES 84
JOLLY GINGER REINDEER COOKIES....203
ORANGE SUGAR COOKIES 108
PASTEL TEA COOKIES....................9
PECAN CUTOUT COOKIES 176
SANTA CLAUS SUGAR COOKIES 198
SCALLOPED MOCHA COOKIES 50
SNOW ANGEL COOKIES 107
SNOWFLAKE COOKIES 96
SPICED GERMAN COOKIES...........195
SPRING GARDEN COOKIE PUZZLE 87
STACKED CHRISTMAS TREE COOKIES .199
STAR COOKIES.........................89
STRAWBERRY VALENTINE COOKIES 86
SUGAR DOVES 93
THICK SUGAR COOKIES.................61
VANILLA-BUTTER SUGAR COOKIES....185
VIENNESE COOKIES....................46
WALNUT CHOCOLATE HEARTS 188
WISHING COOKIES.....................38

DROP COOKIES
BUTTERSCOTCH TOFFEE COOKIES......9
BUTTERY LACE COOKIES 56
BUTTERY POTATO CHIP COOKIES 16
CHOCOLATE CHIP COOKIE MIX.......159
CHOCOLATE-DIPPED ALMOND
   MACAROONS 69
CHOCOLATE-PEANUT BUTTER CUP
   COOKIES 32
COCONUT CLOUDS....................18
COCONUT DROP COOKIES 29
CRANBERRY-CHOCOLATE CHIP
   COOKIE MIX........................164
GIANT MONSTER COOKIES 51
JUMBO CHOCOLATE CHIP COOKIES ...13
NORWEGIAN CHOCOLATE CHIP
   COOKIES 57
OATMEAL RAISIN COOKIE MIX........168
OATMEAL SURPRISE COOKIES 72
QUADRUPLE CHOCOLATE CHUNK
   COOKIES 10
RANGER COOKIES 26
SALTED CASHEW & CARAMEL CHEWS .80
SOFT HONEY COOKIES.................35
SPICY OATMEAL COOKIE MIX.........166
TRIPLE-CHOCOLATE BROWNIE
   COOKIES 62
TRIPLE CHOCOLATE COOKIE MIX 157

MERINGUE COOKIES
CHOCOLATE-DIPPED STRAWBERRY
   MERINGUE ROSES...................99
MERINGUE SANTA HATS...............183
MINT TWIST MERINGUES..............171

MISCELLANEOUS
HAZELNUT CHOCOLATE CHIP
   PIZZELLE 68
PIGGY POPS...........................105
TOM TURKEYS 101

REFRIGERATOR COOKIES
ANY HOLIDAY SPRINKLE COOKIES.....185
CHERRY-NUT COOKIES 26
CHOCOLATE ORANGE
   CHECKERBOARD COOKIES...........16
CORNMEAL LIME COOKIES 71
CRANBERRY SLICES 32
EGGNOG COOKIES....................177
ICEBOX HONEY COOKIES...............43
ITALIAN SPUMONI COOKIES 189
LEMON ANGEL WINGS.................180
LEMON POPPY SEED SLICES 36
LIME SHORTBREAD WITH DRIED
   CHERRIES 62
MINTY WREATHS 174
NANNY'S FRUITCAKE COOKIES 184
OWL COOKIES........................110
PEANUT CHOCOLATE WHIRLS 20
SHORTBREAD.........................29

SANDWICH COOKIES
APRICOT-FILLED SANDWICH COOKIES 190
BERRY-ALMOND SANDWICH COOKIES 179
BUTTERCUPS 11
CHOCOLATE SANDWICH COOKIES....37
CREAM CHEESE DAINTIES 195
CREAM WAFERS 13
HONEY-NUT CHRISTMAS COOKIES....193
LEMON SNOWDROPS 186
PISTACHIO CHOCOLATE MACARONS ...14
RASPBERRY ALMONETTES.............181
RASPBERRY LINZER COOKIES 192
RED VELVET WHOOPIE PIES 64

SHAPED COOKIES
ALMOND BONBON COOKIES..........202
BUTTER BALL CHIFFONS 78
BUTTER SNOWMEN COOKIE 90
CARAMEL APPLE COOKIES............104
CHERRY BONBON COOKIES 19
CHIPOTLE CRACKLE COOKIES 81
CHOCOLATE ALMOND CRESCENTS 66
CHOCOLATE CHAI SNICKERDOODLES..65
CHOCOLATE-DIPPED ANISE BISCOTTI..27
CHOCOLATE MEXICAN WEDDING
   CAKES.............................56
CHOCOLATE PRETZELS.................49
CHOCOLATE REINDEER................94
CHRISTMAS MICE COOKIES...........108
CHRUSCIKI BOW TIE COOKIES.........180
CHUBBY BUNNIES.....................85
COCONUT RASPBERRY COOKIES 45
COFFEE BONBONS 197
COOKIE ANGELS......................95
COWBOY COOKIE MIX................157
CRANBERRY ORANGE RUGALACH 74
DOUBLE-DRIZZLE PECAN COOKIES.....40
EARL GREY TEA COOKIES...............73
FIG & ALMOND COOKIES..............175
FUDGE-FILLED SANDIES................77
FUDGE-FILLED TOFFEE COOKIES 33
GIANT MOLASSES COOKIES 34
GINGER-DOODLES.....................30
GINGERBREAD TEDDY BEARS..........102
HALLOWEEN PEANUT BUTTER
   COOKIE POPS.......................91

COOKIES (continued)
HAZELNUT ESPRESSO FINGERS IN
   CHOCOLATE.........................197
HEDGEHOG COOKIES..................106
HOMEMADE MACAROON KISSES.......70
ICED COCONUT CRESCENTS 171
JOE FROGGERS.........................46
LEMON OATMEAL SUGAR COOKIES ...44
LOADED-UP PRETZEL COOKIES........15
MERINGUE DROPS......................78
MOLASSES COOKIE MIX 165
MOLASSES CRACKLE COOKIES 60
MY KIDS' FAVORITE COOKIES 19
OATMEAL CHIP COOKIES..............53
PEANUT BUTTER COOKIES 23
PEANUT BUTTER CUP COOKIES 169
PEANUT BUTTER-FILLED COOKIES 35
PEPPERMINT STICK COOKIES.........182
PUMPKIN SEED CRANBERRY
   BISCOTTI............................77
SECRET KISS COOKIES 81
SMILING SUGAR COOKIES 92
SUGAR COOKIES......................43
THUMBPRINT BUTTER COOKIES.......23
TRIPLE-GINGER GINGERSNAPS.........76
TRUFFLE-FILLED COOKIE TARTS........58
VANILLA CRESCENTS 53
WASHBOARD COOKIES................70

SPRITZ
BUTTERY SPRITZ COOKIES.............201
CHOCOLATE-DIPPED ORANGE SPRITZ..55

CORNMEAL
CORNMEAL LIME COOKIES 71

CRANBERRIES
CRANBERRY-CHOCOLATE CHIP
   COOKIE MIX........................164

CRANBERRIES (continued)
CRANBERRY EGGNOG CHEESECAKE
   BARS 172
CRANBERRY ORANGE RUGALACH 74
CRANBERRY SHORTBREAD BARS 176
CRANBERRY SLICES 32
MIX FOR CRANBERRY LEMONADE
   BARS 158

CREAM CHEESE (also see
Mascarpone Cheese; Ricotta Cheese)
APPLE CARAMEL CHEESECAKE BARS ..131
CAPPUCCINO BROWNIES..............154
COBBLESTONE BROWNIES............121
CRANBERRY EGGNOG CHEESECAKE
   BARS 172
CRANBERRY ORANGE RUGALACH 74
CREAM CHEESE DAINTIES 195
CREAM CHEESE SWIRL BROWNIES 115
FROSTED BANANA BARS...............117
HOMEMADE MACAROON KISSES.......70
HONEY-NUT CHRISTMAS COOKIES....193
KEY LIME BARS........................135
PEANUT BUTTER SQUARES............139
PUMPKIN CREAM CHEESE BARS 139
RASPBERRY ALMONETTES.............181
RED VELVET WHOOPIE PIES 64
RICH BUTTERSCOTCH BARS...........118
TOFFEE CHEESECAKE BARS 155

CRISP RICE CEREAL
CHOCOLATE-PEANUT BUTTER
   CRUNCH BARS 136
CRISPY STAR POPS....................83

PEANUT BUTTER CRISPY BARS.........126
RANGER COOKIES 26
TOM TURKEYS 101

EGGNOG
CRANBERRY EGGNOG CHEESECAKE
   BARS 172
EGGNOG COOKIES.....................177

FIGS
FIG & ALMOND COOKIES 175

FRUITS (also see individual types)
CREAM CHEESE DAINTIES 195
NANNY'S FRUITCAKE COOKIES 184

GINGER
GINGER-DOODLES......................30
GINGERBREAD MEN....................173
GINGERBREAD SKELETONS.............88
GINGERBREAD TEDDY BEARS.........102
JOLLY GINGER REINDEER COOKIES....203
LAYERED GINGERBREAD BARS........140
TRIPLE-GINGER GINGERSNAPS.........76

HAZELNUTS
FOLDED HAZELNUT COOKIES 48
HAZELNUT CHOCOLATE CHIP
   PIZZELLE 68
HAZELNUT ESPRESSO FINGERS IN
   CHOCOLATE 197
PEANUT BUTTER-HAZELNUT
   BROWNIES 138

HONEY
CHEWY HONEY GRANOLA BARS 113
HONEY-NUT CHRISTMAS COOKIES....193
HONEY-PECAN SQUARES..............118
ICEBOX HONEY COOKIES...............43
SOFT HONEY COOKIES 35

LEMON
BUTTER BALL CHIFFONS 78
COCONUT CITRUS BARS...............126
LEMON ANGEL WINGS.................180
LEMON OATMEAL SUGAR
   COOKIES............................44
LEMON POPPY SEED SLICES 36
LEMON SNOWDROPS 186
MACADAMIA LEMON BARS 143
MIX FOR CRANBERRY LEMONADE
   BARS 158

LIME
CORNMEAL LIME COOKIES 71
KEY LIME BARS........................135
LIME SHORTBREAD WITH DRIED
   CHERRIES 62

MACADAMIA NUTS
MACADAMIA LEMON BARS 143

MAPLE
GLAZED MAPLE SHORTBREAD
   COOKIES............................22

MARSHMALLOWS
ALMOST A CANDY BAR 114
CHOCOLATE-PEANUT BUTTER
   CRUNCH BARS 136
CRISPY STAR POPS....................83
PEANUT BUTTER CRISPY BARS.........126
TOM TURKEYS 101

MASCARPONE CHEESE
(also see Cream Cheese; Ricotta Cheese)
BLACKBERRY CHEESECAKE BARS......132

MERINGUES
(See Cookies, Meringue)

MINT
CHOCOLATE MINT BROWNIES 129
MINT TWIST MERINGUES 171
MINTY WREATHS 174
PEPPERMINT-FUDGE BROWNIE
   MIX................................163
PEPPERMINT STICK COOKIES.........182

MOLASSES
GIANT MOLASSES COOKIES 34
GINGERBREAD MEN....................173
GINGERBREAD SKELETONS.............88
GINGERBREAD TEDDY BEARS.........102
JOLLY GINGER REINDEER COOKIES....203
LAYERED GINGERBREAD BARS........140
MOLASSES COOKIE MIX 165
MOLASSES CRACKLE COOKIES 60
TRIPLE-GINGER GINGERSNAPS.........76

NUTS (also see specific types)
CHERRY-NUT COOKIES 26
CHUNKY BLOND BROWNIES..........128
CINNAMON NUT BARS.................152
HONEY-NUT CHRISTMAS COOKIES ...193
NANNY'S FRUITCAKE COOKIES 184

OATS
BLUEBERRY CRUMB BARS..............150
BUTTERY LACE COOKIES 56
CARAMEL OAT BAR MIX...............169
CHEWY HONEY GRANOLA BARS 113
CHOCOLATE SANDWICH COOKIES....37
COWBOY COOKIE MIX................157
CRANBERRY EGGNOG CHEESECAKE
   BARS 172
GIANT MONSTER COOKIES 51
LEMON OATMEAL SUGAR COOKIES ...44
MY KIDS' FAVORITE COOKIES 19
OATMEAL CHIP COOKIES..............53
OATMEAL RAISIN COOKIE MIX........168
OATMEAL SURPRISE COOKIES 72
OWL COOKIES........................110
RANGER COOKIES 26
SPICY OATMEAL COOKIE MIX.........166
WARREN'S OATMEAL JAM
   SQUARES...........................134

ORANGE
CHOCOLATE-DIPPED ORANGE
   SPRITZ..............................55
CHOCOLATE ORANGE
   CHECKERBOARD COOKIES...........16
COCONUT CITRUS BARS...............126
CRANBERRY ORANGE RUGALACH 74
ORANGE SUGAR COOKIES.............108

PEANUT BUTTER
ALMOST A CANDY BAR 114
CHOCOLATE-PEANUT BUTTER
   CRUNCH BARS 136
CHOCOLATE-PEANUT BUTTER CUP
   COOKIES............................32
GIANT MONSTER COOKIES 51
HALLOWEEN PEANUT BUTTER
   COOKIE POPS.......................91
OWL COOKIES........................110

PEANUT BUTTER BROWNIE MIX.......166
PEANUT BUTTER CAKE BARS 121
PEANUT BUTTER COOKIES 23
PEANUT BUTTER CRISPY BARS........126
PEANUT BUTTER CUP COOKIES 169
PEANUT BUTTER-FILLED COOKIES 35
PEANUT BUTTER-HAZELNUT
    BROWNIES..........................138
PEANUT BUTTER SQUARES............139
PEANUT CHOCOLATE WHIRLS 20
YUMMY COOKIE BARS 146

PECANS
BASIC BROWNIE MIX..................162
CHOCOLATE ORANGE
    CHECKERBOARD COOKIES...........16
CHOCOLATE PECAN PIE BARS.........142
DOUBLE-DRIZZLE PECAN COOKIES.....40
FUDGE-FILLED SANDIES................77
FUDGE-FILLED TOFFEE COOKIES 33
HONEY-PECAN SQUARES..............118
JUMBO CHOCOLATE CHIP
    COOKIES............................13
PECAN CUTOUT COOKIES.............176

PEPPERS
CHIPOTLE CRACKLE COOKIES..........81

PISTACHIOS
ITALIAN SPUMONI COOKIES 189
PISTACHIO CHOCOLATE
    MACARONS 14

POPPY SEEDS
LEMON POPPY SEED SLICES.............36

POTATO CHIPS
BUTTERY POTATO CHIP COOKIES 16

PRETZELS
CHOCOLATE-PEANUT BUTTER
    CRUNCH BARS 136
LOADED-UP PRETZEL COOKIES.........15
TRIPLE-LAYER PRETZEL BROWNIES....122

PUMPKIN
HALLOWEEN PUMPKIN BARS..........109
PUMPKIN BARS WITH BROWNED
    BUTTER FROSTING..................145
PUMPKIN CREAM CHEESE BARS 139
PUMPKIN SEED CRANBERRY
    BISCOTTI...........................77

RAISINS
NANNY'S FRUITCAKE COOKIES 184
OATMEAL RAISIN COOKIE MIX........168
OATMEAL SURPRISE COOKIES..........72

RASPBERRIES
BERRY-ALMOND SANDWICH
    COOKIES............................179
BUTTERCUPS 11
COCONUT RASPBERRY COOKIES 45
RASPBERRY ALMONETTES.............181
RASPBERRY BARS 131
RASPBERRY LINZER COOKIES 192
RASPBERRY TRUFFLE BROWNIES 147
WARREN'S OATMEAL JAM SQUARES ..134

RICOTTA CHEESE
(also see Cream Cheese; Mascarpone
Cheese)
BLACKBERRY CHEESECAKE BARS.....132

SPICE
CHOCOLATE CHAI SNICKERDOODLES..65
JOE FROGGERS.........................46
MOLASSES COOKIE MIX 165
MOLASSES CRACKLE COOKIES 60
SNOW ANGEL COOKIES 107
SPICED GERMAN COOKIES............195
TRIPLE-GINGER GINGERSNAPS..........76
WISHING COOKIES.......................38

STRAWBERRIES
CHOCOLATE-DIPPED STRAWBERRY
    MERINGUE ROSES....................99
STRAWBERRY VALENTINE COOKIES 86

TEA
EARL GREY TEA COOKIES...............73

TOFFEE
BUTTER BALL CHIFFONS 78
BUTTERSCOTCH TOFFEE COOKIES......9
CARAMEL TOFFEE BROWNIES.........153
CHOCOLATE TOFFEE DELIGHTS...123
FUDGE-FILLED TOFFEE COOKIES 33
TOFFEE CHEESECAKE BARS 155

VANILLA
VANILLA-BUTTER SUGAR COOKIES....185
VANILLA CRESCENTS 53

WALNUTS
BUTTERY POTATO CHIP COOKIES 16
CARAMEL-WALNUT STAR COOKIES...196
CHERRY WALNUT SQUARES 149
SUGAR DOVES 93
WALNUT CHOCOLATE HEARTS 188

WHITE CHIPS
(also see Chocolate)
ALMOND APRICOT BARS 144
CHERRY WALNUT SQUARES 149
CHOCOLATE PRETZELS................ 49
CHUNKY BLOND BROWNIES......... 128
CRISPY STAR POPS 83
DIPPED BROWNIE POPS 100
PEPPERMINT STICK COOKIES 182
PIGGY POPS 105
QUADRUPLE CHOCOLATE CHUNK
    COOKIES 10
RASPBERRY BARS 131
RED VELVET WHOOPIE PIES 64
SAND ART BROWNIE MIX 158
TRIPLE CHOCOLATE COOKIE MIX 157
WHITE BROWNIES.................... 148

· Alphabetical Index ·

A
ALMOND APRICOT BARS 144
ALMOND BONBON COOKIES.........202
ALMOND-BUTTER COOKIE BOUQUET..97
ALMOST A CANDY BAR 114
ANISE BUTTER COOKIES...............36
ANY HOLIDAY SPRINKLE COOKIES.....185
APPLE CARAMEL CHEESECAKE BARS .131
APRICOT-FILLED SANDWICH COOKIES 190

B
BASIC BROWNIE MIX..................162
BERRY-ALMOND SANDWICH COOKIES 179
BLACKBERRY CHEESECAKE BARS......132
BLUEBERRY CRUMB BARS..............150
BUTTER BALL CHIFFONS 78
BUTTER SNOWMEN COOKIE 90
BUTTERCUPS 11
BUTTERSCOTCH TOFFEE COOKIES......9
BUTTERY LACE COOKIES 56

BUTTERY POTATO CHIP COOKIES 16
BUTTERY SPRITZ COOKIES.............201

C
CALGARY NANAIMO BARS 122
CAPPUCCINO BROWNIES..............154
CARAMEL APPLE COOKIES............104
CARAMEL OAT BAR MIX...............169
CARAMEL TOFFEE BROWNIES.........153
CARAMEL-WALNUT STAR COOKIES...196
CHERRY BARS..........................148
CHERRY BONBON COOKIES 19
CHERRY-NUT COOKIES 26
CHERRY WALNUT SQUARES...........149
CHEWY CHOCOLATE-CHERRY BARS...113
CHEWY HONEY GRANOLA BARS 113
CHIPOTLE CRACKLE COOKIES..........81
CHOCOLATE ALMOND CRESCENTS ...66
CHOCOLATE CHAI
    SNICKERDOODLES..................65

CHOCOLATE CHIP COOKIE MIX........159
CHOCOLATE-DIPPED ALMOND
    MACAROONS 69
CHOCOLATE-DIPPED ANISE
    BISCOTTI...........................27
CHOCOLATE-DIPPED ORANGE SPRITZ..55
CHOCOLATE-DIPPED STRAWBERRY
    MERINGUE ROSES...................99
CHOCOLATE MEXICAN WEDDING
    CAKES..............................56
CHOCOLATE MINT BROWNIES 129
CHOCOLATE ORANGE CHECKERBOARD
    COOKIES 16
CHOCOLATE-PEANUT BUTTER
    CRUNCH BARS 136
CHOCOLATE-PEANUT BUTTER CUP
    COOKIES...........................32
CHOCOLATE PECAN PIE BARS.........142
CHOCOLATE PRETZELS................49
CHOCOLATE REINDEER...............94

CHOCOLATE SANDWICH COOKIES.....37
CHOCOLATE SAUCE BROWNIES.......119
CHOCOLATE TOFFEE DELIGHTS.....123
CHRISTMAS MICE COOKIES............108
CHRUSCIKI BOW TIE COOKIES.........180
CHUBBY BUNNIES 85
CHUNKY BLOND BROWNIES..........128
CINNAMON NUT BARS.................152
COBBLESTONE BROWNIES...........121
COCONUT CHIP NUT BARS 125
COCONUT CITRUS BARS................126
COCONUT CLOUDS....................18
COCONUT DROP COOKIES 29
COCONUT RASPBERRY COOKIES.....45
COFFEE BONBONS 197
COOKIE ANGELS.......................95
COOKIE DOUGH BROWNIES..........130
CORNMEAL LIME COOKIES 71
COWBOY COOKIE MIX................157
CRANBERRY-CHOCOLATE CHIP
    COOKIE MIX.........................164
CRANBERRY EGGNOG CHEESECAKE
    BARS................................172
CRANBERRY ORANGE RUGALACH 74
CRANBERRY SHORTBREAD BARS 176
CRANBERRY SLICES....................32
CREAM CHEESE DAINTIES 195
CREAM CHEESE SWIRL BROWNIES ...115
CREAM WAFERS.......................13
CRISP SUGAR COOKIE MIX 161
CRISPY STAR POPS....................83

D
DIPPED BROWNIE POPS 100
DOUBLE-DRIZZLE PECAN COOKIES.....40

E
EARL GREY TEA COOKIES...............73
EGGNOG COOKIES.....................177
ELF COOKIES..........................103
EXTRA-SPECIAL CASHEW
    CRESCENTS 41

F
FAVORITE SUGAR COOKIES............191
FIG & ALMOND COOKIES 175
FOLDED HAZELNUT COOKIES 48
FROSTED BANANA BARS...............117
FROSTED MALTED MILK COOKIES 25
FUDGE-FILLED SANDIES...............77
FUDGE-FILLED TOFFEE COOKIES 33

G
GERMAN CHOCOLATE BROWNIES 120
GIANT DINOSAUR COOKIES............83
GIANT MOLASSES COOKIES 34
GIANT MONSTER COOKIES 51
GINGER-DOODLES.....................30
GINGERBREAD MEN...................173
GINGERBREAD SKELETONS............88
GINGERBREAD TEDDY BEARS.........102
GLAZED MAPLE SHORTBREAD
    COOKIES............................22
GOLD RUSH BROWNIES 135

H
HALLOWEEN CUTOUT COOKIES 84
HALLOWEEN PEANUT BUTTER
    COOKIE POPS.......................91
HALLOWEEN PUMPKIN BARS..........109
HAZELNUT CHOCOLATE CHIP
    PIZZELLE 68

HAZELNUT ESPRESSO FINGERS IN
    CHOCOLATE........................197
HEDGEHOG COOKIES.................106
HOMEMADE MACAROON KISSES......70
HONEY-NUT CHRISTMAS COOKIES...193
HONEY-PECAN SQUARES..............118

I
ICEBOX HONEY COOKIES...............43
ICED COCONUT CRESCENTS 171
ITALIAN SPUMONI COOKIES 189

J
JOE FROGGERS 46
JOLLY GINGER REINDEER COOKIES....203
JUMBO CHOCOLATE CHIP
    COOKIES............................13

K
KEY LIME BARS........................135

L
LAYERED GINGERBREAD BARS........140
LEMON ANGEL WINGS................180
LEMON OATMEAL SUGAR
    COOKIES............................44
LEMON POPPY SEED SLICES..........36
LEMON SNOWDROPS 186
LIME SHORTBREAD WITH DRIED
    CHERRIES 62
LOADED-UP PRETZEL COOKIES.......15

M
MACADAMIA LEMON BARS 143
MERINGUE DROPS 78
MERINGUE SANTA HATS 183
MINT TWIST MERINGUES 171
MINTY WREATHS 174
MIX FOR CRANBERRY LEMONADE
    BARS................................158
MOLASSES COOKIE MIX 165
MOLASSES CRACKLE COOKIES 60
MY KIDS' FAVORITE COOKIES 19

N
NANNY'S FRUITCAKE COOKIES 184
NORWEGIAN CHOCOLATE CHIP
    COOKIES............................57

O
OATMEAL CHIP COOKIES...............53
OATMEAL RAISIN COOKIE MIX........168
OATMEAL SURPRISE COOKIES.........72
ORANGE SUGAR COOKIES.............108
OWL COOKIES.........................110

P
PASTEL TEA COOKIES................. 9
PEANUT BUTTER BROWNIE MIX.......166
PEANUT BUTTER CAKE BARS 121
PEANUT BUTTER COOKIES 23
PEANUT BUTTER CRISPY BARS........126
PEANUT BUTTER CUP COOKIES 169
PEANUT BUTTER-FILLED COOKIES 35
PEANUT BUTTER-HAZELNUT
    BROWNIES..........................138
PEANUT BUTTER SQUARES...........139
PEANUT CHOCOLATE WHIRLS 20
PECAN CUTOUT COOKIES.............176
PEPPERMINT-FUDGE BROWNIE MIX ...163
PEPPERMINT STICK COOKIES.........182
PIGGY POPS..........................105

PISTACHIO CHOCOLATE MACARONS ..14
PUMPKIN BARS WITH BROWNED
    BUTTER FROSTING...................145
PUMPKIN CREAM CHEESE BARS 139
PUMPKIN SEED CRANBERRY
    BISCOTTI............................77

Q
QUADRUPLE CHOCOLATE CHUNK
    COOKIES............................10

R
RANGER COOKIES 26
RASPBERRY ALMONETTES.............181
RASPBERRY BARS 131
RASPBERRY LINZER COOKIES 192
RASPBERRY TRUFFLE BROWNIES 147
RED VELVET WHOOPIE PIES 64
RICH BUTTERSCOTCH BARS..........118

S
SALTED CASHEW & CARAMEL
    CHEWS..............................80
SAND ART BROWNIE MIX.............158
SANTA CLAUS SUGAR COOKIES 198
SCALLOPED MOCHA COOKIES 50
SECRET KISS COOKIES................81
SHORTBREAD.........................29
SMILING SUGAR COOKIES 92
SNOW ANGEL COOKIES 107
SNOWFLAKE COOKIES 96
SOFT HONEY COOKIES 35
SPICED GERMAN COOKIES............195
SPICY OATMEAL COOKIE MIX.........166
SPRING GARDEN COOKIE PUZZLE 87
STACKED CHRISTMAS TREE
    COOKIES............................199
STAR COOKIES........................89
STRAWBERRY VALENTINE COOKIES ...86
SUGAR COOKIES......................43
SUGAR DOVES........................93

T
THICK SUGAR COOKIES................61
THUMBPRINT BUTTER COOKIES........23
TOFFEE CHEESECAKE BARS 155
TOM TURKEYS 101
TRIPLE-CHOCOLATE BROWNIE
    COOKIES............................62
TRIPLE CHOCOLATE COOKIE MIX 157
TRIPLE-GINGER GINGERSNAPS.......76
TRIPLE-LAYER PRETZEL BROWNIES....122
TRUFFLE-FILLED COOKIE TARTS.......58

U
ULTIMATE DOUBLE CHOCOLATE
    BROWNIES..........................127

V
VANILLA-BUTTER SUGAR COOKIES....185
VANILLA CRESCENTS 53
VIENNESE COOKIES....................46

W
WALNUT CHOCOLATE HEARTS 188
WARREN'S OATMEAL JAM SQUARES ..134
WASHBOARD COOKIES................70
WHITE BROWNIES.....................148
WISHING COOKIES....................38

Y
YUMMY COOKIE BARS 146